Growing Up Kent

Matthew William Kent

To Mom and Dad, thank you. For everything.

To my brothers Shawn, Jared, and Joe, for a lifetime's supply of laughs.

To my wife, Andrea, for your love and unwavering encouragement.

CONTENTS

PREFACE

I started graduate school in the fall of 2012, eleven years after completing my undergraduate degree. Eleven long years away from academia. Eleven long years of not sending electronic signals to that certain section of your brain that triggers your hand into writing research papers. This decade-plus-long education gap was a shock to my brain. It made my brain wiggle in a very uncomfortable manner; rest assured, it was not wiggling with joy or excitement, it was wiggling with pain.

One thing about graduate school that quickly became apparent was the folks in charge at the school, the folks who stood up in front of the classrooms... those folks expected their students to write papers...a lot of papers. 10-page papers, 20-page papers, 30-page papers...30 pages? Yes, 30 pages. Start writing. The first time one of those professors stood up there and told my class about a 30-page assignment, I snickered and looked around the room like it was some kind of practical joke. "Ha, that old professor got us this time, huh guys? He's such a kidder." This was no joke though, my peers were quickly jotting notes regarding the expectations of said 30-page paper. "This is madness," I whispered to myself. And I was correct in the assumption—it was madness.

The next thing I quickly learned in graduate school was that *'writer's block'* is a real life disease; it's a bona fide mental condition. I knew I would need to discover a way to overcome this bona fide mental condition called writer's block if I was to ever survive graduate school. Through trial and error, which included staring blankly at walls for hours on end, I discovered that the best way to overcome the mental block was to write about things I knew, events I had experienced, and so forth. You know, get the juices flowing, as they say.

Initially I started writing down short snippets of childhood experiences. These were easy to write about on account of I was there and knew what happened. I had firsthand experience of my upbringing, very convenient. Once I started writing about things I knew, I was often able to break the spell of writer's block and get back to the task at hand of writing boring graduate school research papers about Electrical Vehicle Tax Rates or Enron's Impact on the Energy Markets...blah, blah, and more blah.

However, I started coming back to the childhood experience writings more and more and eventually realized that it was slowly becoming a creative outlet. I was actually enjoying writing about the experiences. I no longer needed the writings to break my writer's block, but I was enjoying seeing where the stories would go and what details I could capture.

The stories and memories began to grow and I started putting more and more down on paper. What started as a few small experiences and pages of writings grew into its final form, which is in the following pages.

Writing is an oddly personal experience and I found myself having internal debates on what exactly to do with the "finished" product. There are times when the stories I've written seem fantastic and worthy of sharing and then the same story read a few days later makes me think twice about putting myself out there and letting others read (judge) my work. I have obviously decided on the latter, hoping the judges are not too critical. And, if the judges are too critical then they can just use these writings as kenneling to start themselves a big ol' bonfire...but, just remember what happened the last time people started burning books they didn't care for...this guy named Adolf was running the show then; I won't spoil the ending of that story, but trust me, it's not a positive outcome.

Anyways, the following pages contain stories about growing up in my—our—family. All of the stories are based on events that actually happened. Although some of the surrounding details might be a tad embellished; some are embellished a little...some are embellished a lot, some probably a ridiculous amount...but that's how writing goes. Sometimes you let it take you where it wants; it's all part of the journey. Anywho, without further procrastination and personal rambling, I present to the 'judges': *Growing Up Kent.*

THE POT

A friend once said to me, "Listen man, my family grew up without a pot to piss in...we didn't know any better and quite frankly...we liked it." I have no doubt in my mind they didn't know any better, most likely because they were five years old, but to be perfectly honest, I'm pretty sure they didn't *like it*, per se.

My family was fortunate enough to come of age with a pot to piss in. It was a metal pot that had been painted white. It had a metal handle and a faded old-timey logo on the side. It was literally a pot to piss in—and poop in, if a number two were to arise, which God help you if it did. I said to my friend who had grown up with no pot to piss in, "Listen here pal, I grew up with a pot to piss in, and trust me, it's no cakewalk."

Our pissing pot is now filled with potting soil and a wonderful green plant that has thin vine-like leaves. This plant thrives in the pissing pot to this very day; it has made itself a fine home in that old white pissing pot. The plant that lives in the pissing pot is housed

1

in the bathroom, which is a very appropriate place for it.

Sometimes, when I am using the bathroom where that plant lives, I sit and look at that plant with the thin vine-like leaves and think to myself, *Hey happy green plant, do you have any idea about all the shit you are sitting in? Do you understand that, plant?* The green plant with the vine-like leaves does not understand that, due to the fact that it is, and always will be, a plant, and plants are unable to think or comprehend the English language. I feel bad for that plant, but the plant is happy, and that's all that really matters.

Now this pissing pot wasn't used in our normal home. In our normal home we had a toilet...two toilets in fact. We were toilet rich, so to speak. No, we used this pot at our lake home, in the winter, when it was cold, and metal is cold, especially on unclothed little butt cheeks. Make no mistake, this is a bit disgusting, but we must forge ahead in the interest of painting the picture and telling the story.

You see, back in the olden days (the early 1980s), most lake houses did not have running water in the wintertime. With no running water, there could be no flushing of the toilets unless you were to transport mass quantities of water for flushing your number ones and number twos. That is to say, bring your water from an outside source. In reality, who is going to bring one hundred gallons of water just to go to the lake for the weekend? Nobody, that's who. Now, there were activities and experiences to be had at the lake in the winter months; fun activities like skiing, snowmobiling, ice-skating, pissing...in pots. However, to gain these wintery experiences you had to be a hardy folk, you had to be willing to freeze your buns off, and also willing to use the pissing pot. Well, it just so happened that we claimed to ourselves that we were in fact hardy folks.

On weekend voyages to the lake house in the winter, the family from the normal house would fill up old used milk jugs with tap water for their trips to the lake. Sometimes the water smelled like sour milk, sometimes it did not; this is the world you live in when you transport your water by old milk jug, these are the dice you roll. You learn to live with it, you tough it out. They would pack just enough water for essential uses, most of which seemed to go towards making coffee for the folks in charge of the whole operation.

There was running water year round at the normal home, enough running water to bring a hundred million gallons to the lake house if need be. The family also owned a big tan conversion van that drove them to the lake house. The big tan van could transport a hundred million gallons of water if need be. In terms of capacity and availability, the family could get at all the water they needed for their wintry weekend trips. However, for reasons unexplained, the family did not bring a hundred million gallons of water with them on these cold winter excursions, they didn't even bring one hundred gallons, they brought one; as in singular. One gallon of water stored in an old rinsed-out milk jug. The one gallon of water was all the family could spare apparently. The one gallon of water would have to be enough to get those hardy folks through the weekend at the lake. Rest assured, the one gallon of water was ever enough.

Since there was no running water, potty and poopie breaks were of the 'not-normal' variety on those wintry weekends. The potty part of the equation was usually easy enough, seeing as how the family from the normal house had four boys. Those little fellas would step out into the frigid winter air and just let it fly into the snow, *easy peasy, mac and cheesy* as the saying goes.

The number two-ing was not easy at the lake house, it was not stepping outside and letting it fly. It was hard. It was not pleasant. The taking of a number two was the opposite of fun. The taking of a number two included you and the little metal pot having some alone time behind the little wooden door of the latrine.

The number two evacuations was where the rubber really hit the road, it's where those boys found out if they were one of those hardy folks they claimed to be. To be perfectly honest, number twos took long-term planning. If those boys were going to be successful in their number two-ing, the planning needed to start one or two days in advance of the lake house visits. To be perfectly blunt on the topic, this planning meant no 'loose-stool'-inducing foods. Can you imagine? Can you even imagine? Try not to think about it, but if you must think about it, imagine scarfing down two or three beef enchiladas and a plate of refried beans on the Thursday or Friday prior to a winter weekend visit to the lake house. Are you catching the drift yet? Is this starting to sink into your brain? A plate of enchiladas and refried beans can give you tummy trouble in a normal setting, but tummy trouble at the lake...in the dead of winter...with no running water...can you even imagine? Can. You. Imagine?

Further details regarding the available varieties of

number twos shan't be explored in this space for obvious reasons. However, it was absolutely imperative that before that small wooden door to the latrine was shut, the entrant knew what they were dealing with. This point cannot be emphasized enough. There were to be no surprises in there, there could *not* be surprises. It had to be you, the white pot with the old-timey logo, and a calm confidence of what exactly you were dealing with, what sort of business you were about to enter into.

For the movement of the number two was only the halfway point of this dismal journey. The real trouble of this whole ordeal lay after the movement was finished. For afterwards, after the deed was completed, after all was said and done...came the walk of shame. Taking the fallen soldier back to the forest behind the lake house for disposal. God help you. I mean, God honestly help you if your number two was not of the 'sturdy' variety.

The next indignity those boys faced in this rite of passage was upon returning to the lake house, wanting nothing more than to wash those dirty hands of the filth they had created. "Mommy dearest...oh mother of mine who brought me forth into this cold, cold world...can you spare some water so I may wash away this sin...wash away this filth that has been created..."

"No, rub some snow on your hands," the answer would be, as she sipped her freshly brewed, sour-milk laced coffee.

The final indignity of this whole ordeal lay in the fact that the lake house at the time was fairly limited in space. In the winter months, the living space became even smaller as the heat did not permeate to the second floor. So there the family would be, huddled in two small rooms on the first floor of the lake house, both rooms in clear sight of the small wooden door to the latrine—the latrine that housed the pissing pot. I tell you this only to allude to the fact that everyone present at the lake house, every last one of those hardy folks that had made the journey up north, those hardy folks knew that you were going to experience a number two. There was no hiding it, or beating around the bush.

If you were to stand and make that short walk to the wooden door of the latrine, they knew—everyone knew—you were going in. You were going to have some 'time on the pot', if you will. And maybe those hardy bystanders would say a short prayer for you, pray you had eaten good solid foods, pray you had done your long-term planning and had had a meal that had stuck to your ribs. Maybe they would pray...maybe they would not. Those hardy folks would watch without watching as you made your way. And maybe you would give a small nod to those hardy folks before opening that small wooden door, a small nod before sitting on the little metal pot with the metal handle and old-timey logo on the side. A small nod to say to those other hardy folks, "I'm going in...I know what I'm doing."

THE LABOR FORCE I
(THE EARLY YEARS)

We grew up like most folks grow up, we had some things and we did not have some other things. We were aware of what we had and we envied those things which we did not have, just like everyone else does. Pretty standard growing-up stuff. There was a lake house in the possession of the family, and the cost and upkeep of that additional property deterred the family from having other things we wanted. Sometimes we liked that, and sometimes we did not. We did not like it when we had to do number twos in the dead of winter, with our little butt cheeks on our little white metal pot with the old-timey logo on the side. Our normal house was a good one; we had a bit of land and two toilets that worked all year round. In the summer we had three working toilets between the two properties. We were toilet filthy-rich in the summer months.

There was a happy mother and father that owned the normal house and lake house. Along with the mother and father there were four scrawny boys with knobby knees that filled those two properties; the boys were appropriately named in order of their birth as Number 1, Number 2, Number 3, and Number 4. I was number two in that line...part of the upper class as my elder brother and I would like to claim, not like those unruly folks residing in the Number 3 slot or, God forbid, Number 4 in the birth order. Can you imagine that? Can you even imagine being Number 4? Good luck with that. I was a middle child, but upper-middle if I do say so myself.

The knobby-ness of the boys' knees was of cartoonish proportions. There is no literary description that can aptly capture the condition of these knees, no words can truly describe them, and therefore no attempt at that endeavor will be made. Photographic evidence is the only medium that can accurately portray how knobby the knees truly were. Here is such photographic evidence:

In the photo, it's clear to see the knobby knees as they bulge from the legs of several of the children. Number 1 is the third child from the right—he's standing beside two of the founding members of the band Mötley Crüe. Standing to Number 1's right is the dashingly handsome Number 2; take a moment to revel in his beauty, try not to get lost in it. Number 3 is third from the left and is completely focused on how he is about to absolutely destroy his cupcake. You can almost hear him muttering under his breath: "I'm going to eat you cupcake...I'm going to eat you so hard." Number 3 is also barefoot because he does not own shoes; this is due to the fact that Number 2 has yet to grow out of his shoes and hand them down to Number 3. Number 4 is on the far left and is presently having his knee eaten by a small black and white dog named Wishbone, but Number 4 is the youngest child so everyone is indifferent to the attack. As the pain spreads across the face of Number 4, the other children laugh whilst bits of cupcakes fall from their mouths.

Now that we have introductions out of the way and we have fully explored the knobby-knee issue, we can continue on. The man-portion of the happy couple that filled those two properties came up as a singleton of two fairly well-off parents. As a young man he was tasked with cleaning up the house before the maid came, and to "watching" over the house when his folks went away for the weekend. Pretty tough gig if he does say so himself. He was a good little boy and always did exactly as he was asked, if we are to believe what has been told.

The woman-portion of the happy couple that filled those two properties came up in a strong catholic family of five kids and of course a mother and father. The family scrapped for everything they could and put together enough for a beautiful home and a swimming pool. Grandmother's meals served as a gathering point in the winters. Every meal filled the house with the smell of sautéed onions; this apparently was the basis for every recipe the woman cooked. The swimming pool served as a gathering point in the summers; many a day spent lazing poolside. They were pool rich, so to speak.

Now then, when the first boy was born into this family that possessed a normal house and a lake house, the father thought to himself, *Well, this is OK, I've got a boy, he can do some work in a few years.* This thought is most likely a paraphrase of what was actually going through his head, but knowing my father, like most fathers, like I am now as a father...you see your little boy and you start thinking about all the jobs you can unload onto that poor unsuspecting baby. That poor unsuspecting babe who is still getting birth-goop wiped off of him. This boy is only five seconds old and already you have him picking up sticks and trimming bushes...these are the thoughts, I know them, I've experienced them.

Approximately two years later another boy emerged to that happy couple that fills those two properties. It was I that did the emerging—I had emerged. I was on the scene so to speak, ready for the big show. '*Let's get to work*' were the first words spoken by Number 2, spoken in the delivery room as a matter of fact. The father of those two boys is licking his lips now...thinking about all those chores to be done.

Not wasting any time to build the labor force, 1.5

years later another boy arrives from the exhausted mother. At this point, the father has enough personnel to field a small landscaping crew, open a masonry shop, or possibly just start a small manual labor camp. Regardless, the labor force is growing, yes sir, things are looking up for the father.

A final boy, Number 4, appears two years after the third. The mother, having seen enough of this sort of thing, announces her retirement from the baby-making industry. The following picture shows the retirement party of the Mother of the Labor Force. Number 1 stands off the shoulder of the mother, with his tired arms tucked into his overalls, apparently having just finished up his shift at the 'picking up sticks' factory.

This retirement announcement of mother was much to the chagrin of the man who was quietly amassing the manpower for future projects; he would have to be happy with a four man labor crew. Regardless of the mother's retirement, the father now has a labor force similar in size to some small countries.

The European country of Liechtenstein rings the family to gauge their interest in consulting with the small alpine land in regards to best practices when building a labor force. The mother declines to take the call; she is retired from that sort of thing, and the father is unwilling to share his good fortunes.

If you have not done the math up to this point, or if arithmetic is not your strong suit, here is the final tally: four boys, less than eight years apart...the Labor Force was formally established. An industrial revolution was on the horizon.

While the mother focuses on feeding, clothing, and rearing those four boys with knobby knees, the father is plotting...planning...scheming. This claim of plotting, planning, scheming cannot be factually verified, but I know it in my heart of hearts to be true. I am a father now, I have had the thoughts.

While the happy couple lie in bed before drifting off to sleep at night, the mother wonders what her boys will become when they are full-grown human beings. What will they be like? Who will they marry? How long will their mullets grow? And the father, where do his thoughts drift to before nodding off to sleep? The father thinks different thoughts. The father thinks thoughts of concrete slabs being poured, walls being built, house renovations commencing. His personal industrial revolution is coming, he must continue his plotting...planning...scheming. For the father must be ready when the Labor Force comes of age.

The Labor Force reached peak production capacity in the late 1980s. The eldest, Number 1, was too young to be off gallivanting around with his friends, and the youngest, Number 4, was just old enough to finally be of some use. The father knew his time had arrived, his personal industrial revolution window was now open...it was time to unleash his Labor Force.

The most grandiose projects bestowed upon the Labor Force involved rocks. Lots and lots of rocks. Big rocks, small rocks, ugly rocks, pretty rocks...if there is such a thing as a pretty rock. You see, there were many rocks lying about on this planet we call Earth. Some of these rocks were hidden, some of these rocks were out in the open. These poor rocks had been lying about for years, just lying there, asking to be made useful...begging to be made useful.

The father of the Labor Force saw these rocks and heeded their call. The father knew and understood the pain those idle rocks felt. In a sense, he had become the rock whisperer. The rocks would call to him in their rock voices, as he lay asleep in bed at night. "Father of the Labor Force," the rocks would say, "if you would only gather us we could make something beautiful. We could have some purpose in this otherwise mundane life of being a rock." Most of these poor rocks had been formed in the early cretaceous period of Earth's history and had been waiting eons for the opportunity to do something...anything really. These rocks yearned to be a part of something bigger.

After one particularly moving conversation with the rocks, the father awoke the next morning with a plan. He had been plotting...planning...scheming for years, and now a vision had been provided, the time had come. The next morning, while the family sat eating their breakfast, the father looked up from his newspaper, and in a very hushed tone he decreed to his Labor Force, "I have listened to the rocks, and now it is time. They want...I mean, *I* want us to build a wall."

The wall that was to be built was like most walls; it was to be very wall-like in all its features. The proposed wall was to be a particular type commonly referred to as a retaining wall. In this instance it would retain the hill that the lake house was built on from sliding into the lake, which most people would agree, would be borderline disastrous. This wall was to be 90 degrees square with the ground, with a top and a bottom, and it served and continues to serve its function as a wall to this very day. The unique thing with this wall was that it was to be built with a rock façade. Big rocks, small rocks, ugly rocks, and pretty rocks. The ugly rocks would need to be kept to a minimum though as this rock wall was to be seen by the public.

The rock wall would be on display every single day and every single night. The rock wall would face the lake, and all those happy boaters and lake-goers would be able to judge and comment on the wall for all eternity, as they drove their boats past the wall. This wall would not get the weekends off, or any holidays for that matter. There would be no time for this wall to *let its hair down*, so to speak. The wall was to be very wall-like in this manner, always being a wall and nothing else.

The wall was very dedicated to its cause. The wall would never wake up on a Tuesday and say "hey father of the Labor Force, I'm thinking about knocking off early this Friday and heading to shoot some stick and drink a few brews with some of the neighborhood walls, thoughts?" This wall is not that kind of wall. It is a wall that stands firm in its position, and holds earth and houses back from sliding into the lake.

The difficult aspect about building a wall made of rocks is that you must first acquire all those rocks. Now unless you are familiar with this sort of thing, you might not know, but rocks can be a bit on the pricey side. This is especially true when you are feeding four boys with knobby knees and trying to maintain a normal house and a lake house, what with all the eating and maintaining of toilets and whatnot. With the aforementioned budget constraints noted, one cannot be expected to just go gallivanting about at a rock store buying up all the pretty rocks.

However, there is a particular type of rock that is not expensive, and that type of rock is known as a "free rock." Free rocks are, as the phrase makes abundantly clear, free of charge. If you can find free rocks to build your wall, you can greatly reduce the cost of building your soon-to-be-on-display-24/7, including Christmas and New Year's Day, rock wall. The difficult part in finding these free rocks is that there is no "free rock" store. The *Free Rock Store* would surely go tits-up within weeks of its grand opening on account of not having any revenue, other than selling the occasional Tootsie Rolls and 3 Musketeer bars to parents to shut up their naggy kids.

There are, however, places on this earth that possess free rocks. Many, many, many, many, many, many free rocks. Big rocks, small rocks, ugly rocks, and pretty rocks for that matter. One of the places on this earth that possess free rocks are lakes. Lakes churn out rocks like it's nobody's business. Now, as luck would have it, our lake house just so happened to be built on a lake. We were very lucky in that turn of events.

Now that a free rock depository had been found, the next hurdle to overcome in building a reasonably priced rock wall is you must pay for the labor to harvest all those rocks. Being that it was around the late 1980s, the father needn't drive to the nearest Home Depot or Lowes and find folks waiting outside to be day laborers. The father had day laborers sleeping under the very same roof that he and the mother slept. The Labor Force would be rounded up and utilized to their fullest extent...the dreams of a father had come true.

The Labor Force would spend the ensuing summer casually collecting rocks while they frolicked in the lake. Anytime one of the boys went in for a dip, encouragement would rain down from above, "grab a few rocks while you're in there." The rocks were plentiful, the lake was supplying a bountiful amount, the lake was purging itself of its rock collection. It was a giving lake, and we were a receiving people. All summer long this kept up. The pace of rock collection was steady, but in the end, that easy-going pace was deemed too slow for the man in charge of the operation.

The season for building a rock wall was fading, and the father was getting antsy to get this project underway. Soon, fall and then winter would arrive and the rock wall would have to wait for another season; this was unacceptable. It had been months since the father of the Labor Force had spoken to the rocks and envisioned the rock wall. With the man in charge worried about the pace of collection being too slow, he thought something must be done.

That something that was to be done was an all-out blitz, a rock-blitz, if there is such a thing. A spectacular one-day event to harvest as many rocks as humanly possible. This harvest was to come from the bountiful lake, or if need be, from the dirt and soil of the very hill which the family would be attempting to retain with their soon-to-be-built rock wall.

The rewards promised to the Labor Force for completing the rock-blitz harvest were to be vast; riches beyond their wildest imaginations in fact. For the first time in their brief history, the Labor Force had negotiated to receive monetary compensation for their hard labor. The price for their efforts was set at a staggering $4 per hour of work...straight cash.

Management was being generous with the common worker, willing to shell out some real Washingtons for their concentrated efforts in the rock blitz. The monetary offer whipped the Labor Force into a frenzy, this was life-changing money for those boys with knobby knees. This was enough cheese to buy yourself something nice and think about settling down, maybe getting your own place, who knows, maybe even retiring.

The work demanded by the man in charge was hard and the day chosen for the work was a stifling hot summer day. The boys began their work on the dirt hill, collecting as many decent sized rocks as they could pry out of the loose soil. Once a rock was identified it was picked up, or rolled, depending upon its size, to the rock wall staging area. The pile of rocks growing larger and larger as the day progressed.

The boys would work on the hill until the sweltering conditions of the day became too much, then they would switch to gathering rocks from the lake, to get a bit of refreshment. The lake work was hard though, it included diving underwater and bringing the rocks to the surface. The lake portion of work was slow going, and therefore was only used sparingly to catch short breaks from the hill work.

As the day dragged on, the Labor Force kept themselves entertained with the thoughts of the dollars that would soon be flowing in once they punched the clock...oh yes, those dollars would be flowing, just like this god-forsaken hill into the lake if this rock wall wasn't built soon. Those boys busted their humps all day gathering rocks. Finally a big enough pile of rocks had been gathered to satisfy the wall builder, the big man in charge.

After seeing the size of the rock pile that had been collected, the wall builder gathered his workers, told them to knock off for the day, grab a root beer and a candy cigarette, kick back and relax. And so the boys did, gathering in the shade under the porch, and throwing back a few suds, just like real men after a hard days work.

Meanwhile, the staggering reality of attempting to pay the price tag of the day's work was slowly setting in with the man in charge of the whole operation. When those boys starting talking about the money they were about to receive, the wall builder became dodgy, unwilling to look the members of the Labor Force in the eye. The father of the Labor Force had not anticipated those boys putting in a full eight-hour day of back-breaking rock-gathering work.

When faced with that reality of what the payout would be, he attempted to float a flimsy compromise to the Labor Force—something in lieu of actual dollars. The compromise was as follows: delivery pizza for dinner, on the house...this one's on us, fellas! A full day's worth of work, all the money they were promised, and the end result is management is going to order delivery pizza, from a restaurant that specializes in making pizza.

Can you imagine the audacity of this offer? To this offered compromise, Number 2 jumped up and hollered: "Man, you got yourself a deal...Holy Lord and his son on this earth named Jesus Christ, you've got yourself a goddamn deal, sir boss!" Sign it, seal it, take it to the postman, and deliver it first class. The 2nd in the lineage, which is I, was, and still is, a self-professed pizza enthusiast. Even the term 'enthusiast' is not a strong enough word in fact. Pizza was, and still is in fact, my heroin...it's my addiction.

Normally the household was forced to endure cheap Chef Boyardee homemade pizza, but now...right now...right at this very moment in time, the foreman is telling those boys they are going to get delivery pizza. Not pizza from some guy named George Johnson from New Jersey who's posing as some bullshit chef named Boyardee, but from an actual, real life pizza place. Physically pick up the phone and call a pizza place and have them cook the pizza, and then bring it to the family for consumption...Number 2 was certain he had died during the manual labor portion of the day and had ascended to pizza heaven.

As for the other three members of the Labor Force, Number 1 summed up their feelings on the negotiations as such: "So...we did all this work and they're going to feed us like they pretty much have to?" To that rhetorical question asked by Number 1, I say yes, but maybe you didn't hear, the food is from a real life pizza store. These were the good times (for some of us), that's for damn sure.

Once all the rocks were collected and delivery pizzas consumed, the real work on the wall began, at least for the foreman of the Labor Force. The foreman tactically placed all those free rocks into a large retaining wall. The foreman can be seen in the following picture finagling a rock into its position. Watching the father of the Labor Force complete this task was similar to watching da Vinci paint the Mona Lisa or Michelangelo complete the David...or something very close to that magnitude.

THE LABOR FORCE II
(THE LATER YEARS)

Many, many years later, almost a lifetime of years it seems, a large acreage of land was purchased by the family. Instrumental in this purchase was the father of the normal house—the foreman of the Labor Force. This purchased land was to be developed into a neighborhood subdivision. Folks from all around the world would come to build houses there, in the way folks usually do in neighborhoods. These houses would be newly constructed and equipped with porcelain toilets and such; it was to be a toilet-rich community it seemed.

Upon closing and acquiring the land, the rock whisperer was once again moved by a nighttime calling. The plot of land that had been purchased required that a water line be buried to connect the soon-to-be neighborhood to the city water pipes. Water was needed of course for all those toilets that those new houses would have. These toilets were to be in working order year round so it was imperative that water access was available year round. The water pipeline to connect to the city lines was to run through an expansive field. An expansive field that just so happened to be littered with rocks. Big rocks, small rocks, ugly rocks, and pretty rocks...mostly rocks with the two worst features, big and ugly. A new project beckoned him. The rocks called during the day, they called during the night...especially at night. The rock whisperer was being stirred to action yet again. The Labor Force would be mobilized and put to work on a new project.

These big, ugly rocks all needed moved, on account of that new waterline that was coming through. The folks who were going to come in and bury that new waterline expected a field without a bunch of rocks living in it, so this field needs to be pristine, free of rocks. Now you might ask, could an earth-mover be rented to accomplish this task? A large piece of yellow equipment with a big scooper, used to scoop all those big, ugly rocks up and move them out of the way? Why yes, of course it could, but why? Why use a costly, big yellow piece of equipment when the Labor Force is already assembled and awaiting instruction, *at the ready*.

Similar to the rock wall, this was to be a one-day rock-blitz...CLEAR THE FIELD!!! was the battle call. The battle call was trumpeted from the highest towers (or maybe just enthusiastically from the father to those boys with knobby knees as they ate their Fruit Loops that morning). Either way, today was the day!

The Father of the Labor Force anticipated that the day to clear the field would be a beautiful, sunny, warm, spring day. What the Father of the Labor Force got was not a beautiful, sunny, warm spring day though, it was an Indiana spring day. It was ugly, and it was cold, it was rain of the cats and dogs variety type, it was an abomination. It was a real life Indiana spring day; which, in case you are not well versed in the subject matter, Indiana spring days are more often than not filled with rain and gloom.

In the water line field, there was a large metal dumpster that was to be filled with the big, ugly rocks, and gal-dammit, we're going to get it filled today, rain or shine. Pouring rain, coming down on those boys, with their knobby knees, and soaked hooded sweatshirts. Rain, slicking all of those big, ugly rocks, turning their ugly colors into darker, uglier colors. Rain, turning the field of grass and rock into a field of mud, half a foot deep.

The day was deplorable. There are no words to describe the true deplorable-ness of that day. But this was the day the rock whisperer had chosen, and therefore there was no going back. It was the most brutal one-day task the Labor Force had ever, or would ever, undertake. The day was the culmination of years of conditioning. The father of the Labor Force envisioned this very effort the day Number 1 sprang from the loins of the mother some 17 years prior.

You see, the eldest of the work crew was growing *long in the tooth*, which is a funny way of saying he was getting older. Soon, Number 1, would be the ripe old age of 18, and no longer under contractual agreement with the Labor Force. The father, and the Labor Force, knew this was their magnum opus, a beautiful grand finale, here in the rain and muck and mire.

With mud up to their knees, and rocks appearing and disappearing in the rain, the Labor Force pushed on, nary a complaint rising up. They went about their work, picking, rolling, and pushing those big, ugly rocks into the dumpster.

Unbeknownst to the rocks, they were being pushed into their tomb. For these rocks were bad rocks, not like those pretty, useful rocks that had been collected years earlier to build a beautiful, well-displayed retaining wall at the lake house. Yes sir, these rocks right here, these damn rocks in this god-forsaken mud-caked field are in the way of progress. And excuse me Mr. Bad Rocks, but maybe you didn't hear, or maybe you can't get it through your thick rock-skull, but this right here is the goddamn United States of America, and progress is king. If you're not paving the way, then you're in the way. And right now, right this very minute, right here in this muck, and mire, and rain...we've got us a water line to lay so that good God-fearing men and women can do their number twos in their brand-new porcelain toilets and wash their dirty hands in their sinks in their brand-new neighborhood. So into the dumpster you go, old pal, you and all your ugly rock friends are out of here.

And that was that. The rocks were gone. The Labor Force were crowned kings of the rock-field, even if for just one ugly, cold day, with rain of the cats and dogs variety.

For the second rock project, the Labor Force received actual monetary compensation, no trickery or false promises this time around; although a certain member of the crew was willing to start the negotiations with delivery pizza.

A few smaller-scale rock projects were requested in the years to come, and various members of the Labor Force gladly obliged, knowing that the rock whisperer never truly stops listening to the calling of the rocks—the big rocks, the small rocks, the ugly rocks, and the pretty rocks. The clearing of the field project was the formal end for the Labor Force rock collection business...at least for the original Labor Force.

However, there are times, even to this day, where the foreman of the Labor Force can be seen staring longingly at rocks in the lake...the rocks are waiting...the head of the Labor Force is biding his time...he's thinking of projects, he's thinking of walls...he's waiting, for the 2nd generation Labor Force to be of age, so he can begin anew.

THE BIG TAN VAN

The family that lived in the normal house and lake house had, among their possessions, a very large, tan conversion van. A big, tan, van. It was a glorious vehicle in every sense of the word. The big tan van embodied what it meant to be glorious. The big tan van was big enough to transport a hundred million gallons of water if need be. The family only transported one gallon at a time though, transporting anything more would just be showing off, and nobody likes that.

Prior to the big tan conversion van, the family was forced to use station wagons for transporting everyone. Shudder the thought, those were the dark ages for sure. No home air conditioning, no dishwashers, and forced to drive around in station wagons? What kind of people were we, savages? Those times we do not speak of. For now...now, we own a big tan conversion van.

The direct impact on the happiness of the family related to the big tan van can be seen in the following chart which plots happiness in terms of before and after owning the big tan van. It is clear to see the vehicle made a lasting impact.

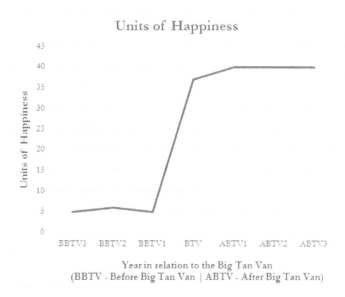

Units of Happiness

(BBTV - Before Big Tan Van | ABTV - After Big Tan Van)

The big tan conversion van had a brown horizontal stripe in the middle to break up the monotony of all that tan. Because really, who wants an all-tan van? Nobody, that's who. The brown stripe was like a dividing line for the van. Up here, above the big brown line, that's the top of the van. The top of the van contained such features as a windshield, windows, a radio antenna, and a luggage rack. Down there, below that big brown line...that's the bottom half of the van. The bottom half contained all the wheels and brakes and such; things that make the big tan van go and stop. That's just the way they painted those vans back then in the olden days, in the 1980s. It was a very stylish era, what with all their solid lines and over usage of tans and browns.

The above picture captures the rear-end of the Big Tan Van, in all its rear-end beautifulness. While the picture is in black and white, allow your mind to fool you into seeing the tan-ness that the van displays...notice the brown-striped-ness of its midsection...notice the ladder to access the top, pretty sweet feature. Also notice the two middle-aged Asian women standing behind the boys with knobby knees...who are they? It doesn't matter who they are, they came all the way to America to get a picture with those three boys, the big tan van, and one ninja warrior, who can be seen on the far left of the picture wearing a tradition ninja headband.

The big tan conversion van had all the conveniences of a modern-day home—with the exception of television and water and those types of necessities. Need to kick back after a rough day at the office? The seats in the big tan van recline. Need to take a nap in the middle of a drive? The back seat bench converted into a bed, for your resting pleasure. Need to transport a hundred million gallons of water? We could, but we shouldn't, the neighbors might talk.

The creature comforts on the inside of the van spared no expense, they were absolute luxury. Velvety cloth seats and cushions that surrounded your body as you sank into them, it was riding in style. The interior of the van was broken up into three very distinct sections. First was the cockpit; this is where the captain and his navigator ran the big show. In the cockpit, coffee was drunk, wheels were steered, radios were tuned, directions were given—very standard driving affairs going on up there in the cockpit.

The next section was referred to as first class. This section was typically reserved for the upperclassmen of the family lineage; you know, the elder statesmen, the distinguished passengers. Meaning of course the eldest and second eldest, Number 1 and Number 2, which was I.

The first class section featured individual bucket seats resting on a swivel with reading lights above each seat. This was commuting in pure luxury for sure. Each seat in first class also had a cloth pouch for storing your wares. Plenty of space was afforded to the first class folks so they didn't need to check any of their luggage. It's just not right to make those first class passengers stow their wares where they can't reach them, I mean, come on, let's be real. Seatbelts in first class were completely optional of course once cruising speed was reached. Actually, seatbelts were optional the whole time in the big tan van. This was the wild west of the late 1980s, after all.

The final section that was available for seating was

coach seating. This was in the butt-end of the big tan van. Coach was where the wild things were kept; the unwashed masses. The 3rd and 4th in the lineage were usually assigned to coach and things were unregulated back there, yes sir, no rules at all back there in coach.

Coach was a good 100 feet away from the cockpit and therefore the flight crew of the big tan van didn't know, and quite honestly, didn't care about what was going on back there in coach. Coach consisted of a long bench seat with a few seatbelts thrown in there for the illusion of safety. The seatbelts never matched up and that was fine, because back there...back there in coach, there ain't no laws, man. Seatbelts? What for? How is one supposed to move about the cabin if one is tethered to their bench? No thanks on the seatbelts.

Coach seating also offered a table smack dab in front of the seating bench. You know, in case those wild folks back there wanted to get an illegal game of slapjack going. Maybe see if the folks from first class might swivel those big comfy first class seats around and try their luck at a game of chance? "Whaddaya say, first class passengers? Feeling lucky??? Want to put that big old allowance of yours on the betting line?"

Coach was designated as a "No Smoking" section just like the rest of the big tan van. However, if one of those wild folks back there were ever to just kick back and enjoy themselves a nice refreshing pull off of a Kool Mild cigarette, if ever that sort of behavior would fly, would pass the mustard, so to speak...it would happen back in coach; where the wild things rode.

The big tan van transported the family and our

one gallon of water to the lake house, where we could piss and number two in our pot if need be. A quick 45-minute drive up the highway was all it took to arrive at the lake house. However, to those youngsters in first class and coach, the 45 minutes of drive time seemed to approach 7-8 hours' worth of real time. It was excruciating for those boys, painful almost. Passing the time became a challenge for those youngsters, and that leads us to where we are really heading with this discussion of the big tan van.

Through sheer boredom and just generally messing about, the wild folks in coach eventually discovered that their side windows could be opened ever so slightly without alerting the flight crew of the big tan van. The big tan van had large rectangle windows along the sides, and those windows had a very small section of them towards the bottom that could be opened. The opening of the windows was a major discovery to those youngsters looking to pass the time. To those coach passengers, this discovery was on par with scientists mapping the human genome. To say it was a huge discovery would be an understatement. With the ability to open a window, the option for activities increased at least tenfold, if not more. Those boys didn't know right away how this discovery would benefit them, but they had a feeling that something good would come of it. Something that would help pass the time on those long, arduous journeys of 45 minutes.

Shortly after the discovery of the opening windows, the folks who received coach tickets on the big tan van began taking a sudden liking to carrots. Now I'm not talking about the big, long, *'Bugs Bunny munching on carrots talking to Elmer Fudd'* variety of carrots, nope, I'm talking about baby carrots. Little, infant-like carrots.

Those coach passengers started requesting baby carrots for the long drive to the lake house. The liking of carrots during the drives to the lake directly coincided with the discovery of the ability to open the little side windows. This is not a coincidence. This here, as a statistician would say, is a direct correlation; one occurrence is directly related to the other. The flight crew was happy to oblige with the carrot request, even if they were a bit naive about the whole thing: "Those nice little boys back in coach are requesting baby carrots again, such health-conscious little fellas they are."

Now, carrots are a solid vegetable, rich in beta-carotene and fiber; aids in the digestion in the animals that consume it and such. Carrots are also there to help all the little bunnies of the world from having to get prescription glasses, if you're inclined to believe this sort of thing. Regardless, the coach passengers suddenly craved the carrots, loved the carrots, couldn't get enough of the darn carrots. But only the baby carrots please.

However, the baby-carrot cravings were confined to their presence in the coach section of the big tan van. The man of the house would say, "Going for a ride in the Buick, you boys want some carrots? I know how you boys love to eat carrots when we're out driving." "No thanks" would be the response from those boys. Always would be, and always was. No attempt at covering up the carrot correlation was made, because that would mean eating carrots, and to be real, who does that? Nobody.

The boys riding coach were not interested in the

health of their bowels, or their levels of beta carotene that the carrots provided. No, those boys didn't care about those trivial, adult benefits associated with carrots. The only thing those boys back in coach cared about was the way those carrots would bounce and dance on the highway after they were pitched out those little open side windows. In case you have been absent for most of your adult life, carrots are a very sturdy vegetable and don't break up to easily when hitting the highway at a high speed.

Other, weaker vegetables, would disintegrate upon touching the asphalt while cruising at a speed of 55 miles per hour. Gone. Poof. Broccoli? Come on, give it a rest already. Broccoli would be torn to shreds. But carrots? Very sturdy. One of the more sturdy veggies one can think of, outside of celery that is, which most would agree is probably the sturdiest vegetable of them all.

The coach folks would launch those baby carrots portside and then watch them bounce along the highway. Boing. Boing. Boing...on down the highway. Baby carrots were a very good highway-bouncing vegetable on account of they are somewhat pliable yet sturdy. While celery might be more sturdy, celery would most likely just skid on the highway. And let's be honest with one another, a stalk of celery skidding on the highway is not nearly as enjoyable as a carrot going boing, boing, boing, on down the highway.

After the baby carrot was launched, the coach passengers would quickly turn and look out the back window and watch those little baby carrots boinging down the road...almost keeping up with the big tan van for a short period of time before tumbling off to the shoulder of the road or getting disintegrated by a semi tire. After they turned to watch, the giggling would start. And then more giggling. Oh the giggling...constant stifled giggling. Like a pack of little schoolgirls back there in the coach section of that there big tan van. Very immature to be quite frank. Quite unlike those sophisticates in first glass sipping their apple juice with pinkies firmly extended. Yes sir, those folks back in coach are an odd lot—what with their baby carrot bouncing and stifled giggling. Very unsophisticated.

The carrot bouncing passed the time for the folks assigned to coach. And they had a good run of it, passing the time with carrot tossing for many a trip to the lake house. This ruse went on for quite a while, until apparently one day the co-pilot of the big tan van became aware of the whole enterprise. The co-pilot must have spotted a baby carrot skidding down the highway and finally put two and two together, And on that day, the jig was up. And when the jig was up, it was up. The jig was not down, it was most definitely up, and high time it was. It was over and that's all there is to it. No more baby carrots. No more nothing. There were no punishments handed down to those couch passengers, and no trouble to be in, simply put, the baby carrot market went dry. The flight crew put an end to the in-flight meal service, especially for any carrot requests.

From that day forward, no more carrots boinging down the road. It was back to the drawing board for passing the time on those long 45-minute journeys. "Say...you folks in first class interested in a little three card monte?" Yes sir, we had it pretty rough on those 45-minute drives after the baby carrot embargo of the late 1980s.

CLOTHING PART I

Clothing the Labor Force was a constant battle for the mother of the happy couple that filled those two properties. As the father lay awake thinking about rock projects and retaining walls, the mother most likely could not sleep due to the worrisome thought of outfitting four rough-and-tumble boys.

The first, and always most reliable, method of outfitting a large squadron of young boys is the old tried and true hand-me-down method. "Hey Number 1, I like that shirt you're wearing." "Great, it'll be yours next year, Number 2." This is how the cycle works. But there is a problem with this cycle, a little issue if you will. The clothing introduced into the cycle only lasts for so long with those rough-and-tumble boys. Therefore, the hand-me-down clothing cycle ends up disjointed and eventually, if it's pushed too far, the cycle breaks down altogether; just like the little cotton fibers holding that Fruit of the Loom undershirt together.

When pushed to the limit, the actual hand-me-down clothing cycle ends up looking something like this: Number 1 gets new clothes, Number 2 gets used clothes from Number 1, Number 3 gets scraps of cloth that once were clothes worn by Number 1 and Number 2...and what does Number 4 get? For all his efforts of showing up last to the big show, for coming late to the party? What does poor Number 4 get? Number 4 gets new clothes of course. Perish the thought of the baby, Number 4, having to wear those scraps of cloth that are dangling off the bones of Number 3.

In case you are having difficulty following the intricacies of the hand-me-down cycle to this point, here is a brief recap: Number 1 and Number 4 get new clothes, Number 2 gets old clothes, and Number 3 gets a scrap piece of cloth and encouragement to cover himself up. "Put on your fanciest rags Number 3, we're going to church to worship the Jesus...oh, let me help you with your bowtie Number 4, you look so handsome with your new tuxedo Number 4, we love you Number 4, Jesus thinks you look so handsome."

Now this is how it was, this was the way it goes, so to speak. Deal with it, we're hardy folks, right? We piss and leave number twos in metal pots for god sakes, certainly we can wear a few rags on our bones here and there.

So, as it were, the boys had very little control over the clothes they wore. However, those boys did have control over one thing that they wore, and that thing that they controlled was shoes, you know...clothing, for your feet.

Shoe shopping happened but once a year, during back-to-school shopping. Now, in the case of young boys, and by young boys in this instance I mean those older than 3rd grade, shoes are everything. And I do mean everything, there is no playing fast and loose with terminology here, a boy's shoes mean everything to him. Everything.

A young boy's shoes are like a young man's car. The shoes are your set of wheels, they're what you show off to your pals, they're how you envision yourself picking up that dame from 4th grade. You roll up to that pretty girl with the yellow ribbons in her hair, you're wearing your brand-new Nikes: "Hey sweetie pie, wondering if you want to share a chocolate snack pack or something…" This is how it goes down in young boys' minds; I know, I have had the thoughts. Without those brand new Nikes though, that previous conversation with the dame from 4th grade is a definite no-go.

Now then, it's established that to young boys, shoes are everything. The problem is, there are budget constraints, there always are and always will be budget constraints. The family just used free labor and free rocks to build a damn retaining wall, do you think the freshest pair of Reebok Pumps are coming in the pipeline for those boys? If you think the answer is yes, stop reading and return to Page 1 and begin anew, for you are sorely mistaken, my friend. The answer on those new Reeboks is a resounding "no."

The first stop in the attempt to purchase shoes for the first day of lessons was Kmart, always with the Kmart. This was always stop one, the boys knew, the mom knew, Kmart knew. This ritual played out year in and year out, load up all those boys in the big tan van and head on over to Kmart for round one of the shoe-buying fight. The problems with the Kmart shoe department are vast and cannot be fully explored in this limited space, but it mostly boils down to their selection, or lack thereof..

The Kmart shoe department is especially troublesome to a young boy looking to secure his set of wheels to pick up all those hot elementary school dames. Kmart offers shoes with names such as TR5800 and KL22; what are these even, just random letters and numbers thrown together? Who wants that on their shoes? If you're looking for the Nike or Reebok section at Kmart you're in the wrong store, pal. In the world of young boys, the aforementioned Kmart shoes with names like TR5800 are commonly referred to as 'Buddies'. Apparently, Kmart had the market cornered on the shoe variety known as Buddies.

Now, in most cases you might be thinking to yourself, *'Great, buddies is a good thing. Bob from accounting, he's my buddy, right?'* Wrong. 'Buddies' in this instance means very bad, very cheap shoes. Now you might be asking yourself, why does the term 'Buddies' mean cheap shoes? Who knows? It's really not important at this point, just grasp it and stop asking so many damn questions. Just understand that a young boy wearing Buddies to elementary school is the equivalent of showing up to your high school prom date's house on a tandem bicycle. Have fun with that. Good luck getting lai... I mean, good luck getting to prom on time.

That sweetie from 4th grade with the cute yellow ribbons in her hair isn't going to come near you with Buddies on your feet...it's not happening. Forget your charm, forget your personality, forget your good looks—if you show up to the first day of school in Buddies, you are done for. Period. End. Of. Story.

Herein lies the rub, the big problem if you will. All mothers that live on the big blue planet like Buddies, mostly because Buddies are cheap. All boys that live on the big blue planet feel a deep repugnance for Buddies, mostly for the same reason moms like Buddies; they're cheap.

Those boys with knobby knees were no different in this regard. They hated Buddies, and they hated that every year, the first stop on the shoe shopping tour was Kmart. Those boys were cunning though, and over the years, they had developed a secret weapon that they deployed when shoe shopping at Kmart.

Every year, their poor mother endured the same song and dance on their annual trip to Kmart. Boy with knobby knees: "Mom, I like these Buddies, they look really, really cool and all...definitely can see getting some girls attention in these...it's just that...well...they *feel funny on my feet is all.*"

'Feel funny on my feet'...did you catch it? That's the secret weapon they deployed. Same line, year in, year out. 'Feels funny on my feet'.

You see, semantics about the coolness of the shoes could be argued endlessly between mother and boy, but how the shoes actually felt on their feet? There's no real good counter-argument for that. Feeling is a personal experience for the wearer of the shoes and mother cannot experience what the shoes feel like to the little feet wearing them. So, no matter what, no matter even if those Buddies felt like the Virgin Mother Mary herself was giving the boy a foot rub with lavender oil, the following words had to be muttered: "These Buddies feel funny on my feet, Mom." Again, there is no counter argument here.

Mother would sigh...the sigh was her will to fight leaving her body, a crack in the armor. It was the boy's job to pry that crack in the armor open. With that sigh, the first battle in the war for shoes had been won...on to round two: onto the Shoe Carnival.

Shoe Carnival is insane. There is no other way to describe this place. Shoe Carnival was insane back then, it is insane now, and it forever shall be, insane. It is a carnival...for shoes. Shoe Carnival has an emcee. Read that line again if you will. An emcee. What kind of shoe store has, or needs for that matter, an emcee? Shoe Carnival, that's who, don't question their business practices. Shoe Carnival also featured a big circular spinning board that you got to spin for discounts or free prizes. What's not to like about this place, it uses the word 'carnival' after all, and who's ever had a sour time at a carnival? Nobody. Well, except for moms with Buddy-hating boys.

The other asset in Shoe Carnival's possession was real shoes—Nikes and Reeboks, and for crying out loud, they even had Adidas. Adidas!?! Maybe this year would be the year?! Who knows? Shoe Carnival was expensive though; this wasn't like the Free Rock Store just giving their inventory away.

Once the family arrived at the Shoe Carnival, those boys scratched and clawed to get name-brand shoes. They pleaded and begged, made promises they had no way of fulfilling, just to get a name brand on the side of those shoes. It meant everything to them, it was their livelihood.

Once those boys got Mother into Shoe Carnival it was name-brand shoes or bust, there was no going back, and they knew it. To add to the pressure of the situation, if the boys took too long shopping at Shoe

Carnival, threats from the clothing provider of returning to Kmart would begin to bubble to the surface.

The imposing of a time limit only added to the madness and intensity of shoe shopping at the Shoe Carnival. The emcee is yelling about sales in aisle two, mother is bearing down on those boys to find some shoes, music is blaring in the background, the spinning prize board is spinning around...tick...tick...tick, threats of packing up and heading for the Buddy store are starting to be muttered more frequently by the clothing lady. This is real life pressure, this is some real world shit right here. (My adrenaline is kicking in just thinking about the pressure-packed shopping that the Shoe Carnival trips provided and I'm forty years old.)

Number 2 and Number 3 fought especially hard for name-brand shoes, any name brand would do honestly. This fight for Number 2 and 3 was more pronounced for several reasons; one reason was that this would be the one new piece of clothing that Number 2 or Number 3 would get that year, the other reason was Number 1 really didn't care all that much about his shoes, and Number 4 got whatever shoes he wanted, because "we don't want our baby to have ugly shoes now do we?"

On one pressure-packed trip to the Shoe Carnival, Number 3 foolishly settled for a pair of all-black Reeboks simply because they said Reebok on the side of them. Number 3 had settled early in the Shoe Carnival trip; he found the first pair of Reeboks with a reasonable price tag and nabbed them. It was a calculated risk on his part, but he removed himself from the pressure of coming down to the wire and having a pair picked for him by the lady in charge.

Those Reeboks that Number 3 picked were not athletic Reeboks by any stretch of the imagination. Deion Sanders or Reggie Miller would not be appearing in any sports advertisement donning these particular black Reeboks any time in the next half century; unless of course Deion Sanders suddenly switched genders and became a waitress at Cracker Barrel. The black Reeboks chosen by Number 3 were less sleek than the orthopedic shoes worn by your grandmother or an elderly nurse. These were Reebok shoes in name only. Did they feel funny on his feet? Who knows, who cares? Number 3 had him some Reeboks and might just have a chance with that sweetie from 4th grade, or so he told himself.

The purchase was made and Number 3 was removed from the pressure cooker that was Shoe Carnival. But, upon arriving at home…the more Number 3 looked at those shoes, the less he felt like a member of the cool kids' club and more like a member of Club Med. After thorough inspection and mulling it over for a few hours, Number 3 finally spoke up—the shoes would have to go back to the Carnival. He just couldn't do it, couldn't wear these orthopedic nurse shoes to school, Reebok or not

After furious debate with the lady in charge, it was decided that the shoes would be returned to their life at the Carnival. This was a very risky move by Number 3; probably one of the most daring moves ever made by Number 3 to be perfectly honest. Number 3 was tempting fate and putting his future back into the hands of the Carnival. He was like an adrenaline junkie that just couldn't get enough of the action.

The other boys looked at him as if he was crazy. "You can't go back in there man," Number 4 said. "You got Reeboks, can't you just be happy and walk away." But Number 4 didn't fully grasp Number 3's plight. Plus, Number 3 was feeling lucky, Number 3 was shootin' for the moon, he was thinking this would be his year.

In the end though, he played it perfectly. Number 3 walked out of the Shoe Carnival with his head held high, a shoe box carrying a brand-new pair of Nikes tucked triumphantly under his arm. He had won the battle; this was mainly due to the sheer exhaustion on the part of the shoe purchaser, who by this point in the ordeal, simply caved to Number 3's demands. The will to fight had been extinguished by the long day at the Carnival. The armor of the shoe purchaser had not only been cracked, it had completely fallen off. Number 3 had played the shoe-buying game flawlessly that year, but the stress of those events most likely weakened his heart and will probably take years off his expected lifespan. After all was said and done though, having those Nikes was most likely worth it to him.

Not all of the knobby kneed crew fared as well as Number 3 did though. On one particular shoe buying trip in the middle school years, Number 2, which is I, stumbled upon a pair of Nikes marked at a deep discount at the Carnival of Shoes. Shoe Carnival wanted these Nikes gone, and they wanted them gone yesterday. Number 2 was coming up against the 'return to Kmart time deadline', and so he grabbed those puppies and held onto them for dear life until the purchase had been completed.

Similar to Number 3's purchase of his black orthopedic Reeboks, Number 2 paid no attention to the finer details of the shoes. They were Nikes at a low price, that was all the detail he needed...sold. Those Nikes felt funny on his feet though. Those shoes fit as poorly as a shoe can fit, with soles as flexible as two-inch plywood. Those Nikes he had bought were not shoes, they were slabs of wood covered in canvas with the name 'Nike' stitched on the side.

After the other boys had made their purchases, the family piled into the big tan van to return home. On the way home, the shoe purchaser sighed and gave a frown as she looked at the receipt. "Number 2," she said, "Number 2, we've got ourselves a bit of an issue here with those brand-new Nikes." She said this in a very hushed tone so those wild folks back in coach seating couldn't hear the conversation. "Number 2, those foot bags masquerading as Nike shoes that we just bought you...those Nikes that you love so much, those Nikes...they're women's shoes." Women's. Shoes worn by females. There it was, and there it is. The caveat. The catch-22.

Number 2 had finally succeeded in getting his name-brand, dame-attracting shoes, and luck be damned if they're actually women's shoes.

Number 2 was quickly presented with two choices by the lady in charge: return to the unknown, into the shoe abyss, back to the old Shoe Carnival and throw his fate to the shoe purchaser...or...or, he could keep his women's Nikes and not tell anyone they're womens. Sweep this whole affair under the rug, a little secret between mother and child. This was a life-altering decision and it was to be made in a moment's notice, no time for delay.

Number 2 stared out the window of the big tan van…the madness of Shoe Carnival flashing before his eyes…the echo of the emcee still bouncing around in his ears. Number 2 cradled the shoebox holding his Nikes like it was suddenly a deformed newborn child. The response came quietly and calmly and without hesitation: "No-no, we're keepin' these," as he patted his shoebox holding those pathetic Nike foot bags. These were Nikes, these were *his* Nikes, his golden ticket.

At school that year, Number 2 spotted another boy wearing the exact same women's Nikes. Nike had apparently made two pairs of these shoes and then decided to scrap the whole project, for obvious reasons. This other boy wore on his feet, the same mess of canvas and plywood claiming to be Nike footwear, for the fairer sex.

The two boys glanced at each other's shoes and at each other. A nod was exchanged between the two boys. A nod so slight it passed in an instant and was seen by no other soul, save the two boys and the Lord above Jesus Christ, who sees all. This other boy knew, they both knew. They were brothers of the same war, had been on the same battleground. The bags under his eyes showed the weariness and intensity of trips to Kmart and the Shoe Carnival. These two were brothers of a solemn oath. Brothers of an exclusive club, *The boys who wear women's Nikes club*. Membership: two. Girls present at club meetings: zero. This was a club that did not have the problem of being pursued by women, or girls as it was.

CLOTHING PART II

Another aspect in the continual war of the clothing of those boys with knobby knees was that they almost instantly destroyed any clothing they received, like most boys do. On the ground, in the trees, in the muck and mire, in creeks, everywhere on God's green earth these boys, all boys, trudge on. Their mission? To destroy clothing, plain and simple, easy as pie. They came here to destroy clothing, and by-golly, they're going to get it done. As Julius Caesar once famously orated back there in Rome, "*Veni, Vidi, destructum vestimentum*"; which translates, roughly, to '*I came, I saw, I destroyed clothing*'.

The mother of those boys understood their mission, she got it, so to speak. She understood their plight as a people. But just because Mother understood their plight doesn't mean she liked it or didn't fight back—on the contrary. She was a general on the other side of the fighting, lined up against the enemy; and fight did she ever. Like an old stubborn mule. She fought back with sew-on patches, or stitching, or prayers...anything really. These were all useless strategies, like trying to use a five-gallon bucket to bail out the sinking Titanic, a hopeless fight really.

Oftentimes, after defeat was imminent, after there was no possible way for her to salvage a piece of clothing, she implored her final line of defense: denial. The mother would flat out refuse that a particular clothing garment was worn out. Plain out lie to herself, even if just for a little while, stretching the lifespan on those garments, even if just for a few days. Sweatpants were her favorite clothing for this brand of trickery—denial.

Understand that sweatpants from the 1980s were not the cool, hip-folk wearing sweatpants of the current times. Sweatpants back then fit weird and looked trashy, real trashy. There was no getting around this fact. There was no such thing as 'dressy-sweats' back in the olden days of the 1980s. No sir, sweatpants of that era were for playing and roughhousing in, and nothing else. So, those boys beat their sweatpants to hell and back. By the time they were done with them, those sweatpants begged to be released from their worldly duty, they begged to be turned into washrags to clean and dry the family station wagon, or the big tan van. "Please," those sweatpants would say, "please, I can't roughhouse anymore; can I clean some tires on that there big tan van? Looks easier than another day of rolling around in the muck and mire."

Sweatpants were also cheap, way cheaper than Wrangler jeans. Mother really liked the cheapness of sweatpants; they had a price she could live with. So, here you go boys, wear these trashy sweatpants outside to destroy. And destroy they did. After awhile, the fabric around the knees would start to thin out, growing more transparent everyday. Holes would quickly appear after that, starting small, seemingly growing by the minute until finally gaping holes appeared in the knees. What started as a pin prick in the sweatpants on Monday would be large enough to fit your hand into by Wednesday and by Friday those holes would be large enough to drive the big tan van through. Those knobby little knees would be on display for the whole world to see.

Now the problem arises: what to do with these trashy sweatpants with gaping holes in the knees? "Look here Ma, I've got these trashy gray sweatpants with two huge holes in them, going to need to trade these puppies in for some new ones." Trade-in? New? Two phrases not often heard or approved of around these parts, unless of course you're Number 4, then by all means sir, please come over here to our new sweatpants section. Trade-in? New? Yeah right. You must be new around here if you're asking for those things. Don't worry though, there's a solution for your little problem, a quick fix, as they say. Take those trashy, gaping-hole sweatpants off, turn them around 180 degrees and slide those things back on your little bottoms. Turn those sweatpants around, you know, wear them backwards. Revolutionary.

With your backward sweatpants, you now have two new layers of fabric to ruin, plus—and this is a big plus of the 'wearing holey clothing backwards method'—you now have ventilation for the back of your knees. Now, please don't sit there with the back of your knees sweating and tell me that you've never thought to yourself how nice it would be to have

48

holes in the back of your pants. Imagine how happy your kneepits would be if they had holes for ventilation.

This next phrase was actually said by the lady in charge of the clothing operation regarding the holes in the back of the pants: "You've always wanted air conditioning, right? You said it yourself that you wanted air conditioning, so there you go."

This was actually said in real life by the lady in charge. "You've always wanted air-conditioning, right?" The author assures you that this quote has not been fabricated or elaborated on, sometimes the material writes itself. This is such demented, twisted, taunting language, it was flat out denial of the truth. This was not air conditioning of the type where you install a window unit here and there to cool a residential property; this was gaping holes in the back of your pants type of air conditioning. This was a whole new level of cheapness in the clothing industry.

Mother was way before her time it seems. At the end of the day though, it's the only air conditioning you're getting, deal with it and embrace it...just don't let anybody see you wearing your portable air conditioning units and sweat-free kneepits.

Other fights related to clothing of the boys were short lived and not nearly as fiery or drawn out as shoes or sweatpants. One particular instance lasted but a few moments, however, it laid down the law in regards to what those boys with knobby knees would put up with and what they would let slide.

In this incident, the lady in charge of clothing the boys brought home a great big bag of shame. A bag so full of shame that its contents had to be hidden in a black garbage bag. No see-through garbage bag for this surprise, lest someone see what was truly hidden within.

The clothing provider knew she had made a mistake the moment she entered the house with the black garbage bag full of shame. Those boys put down their Legos and turned to stare at the clothing provider. They picked up on the fear...they could almost smell it on her, they saw it in her eyes, they saw it in the way she cautiously entered the room, and they saw it in the way she wouldn't look at them straight as she started explaining the wonderful things stowed away in this black garbage bag. Her hands betrayed her as they continued to nervously tighten their grip on the black garbage bag as she prattled on about its contents. In this act, she was the anti-Santa Claus, attempting to deliver shame and embarrassment to all the good little boys of the world.

Those boys might not have been the brightest stars in the night sky, but they knew something was up from the moment she entered carrying that black garbage bag. The clothing lady knew it was a bad idea from the word go, and yet here she was, still walking into the lion's den...hoping and praying that this ruse would succeed.

The black garbage bag of shame that the mother brought forth contained clothes from a friend's son. How nice of that friend, providing hand-me-down clothes to us, very thoughtful, a mighty big thanks. When the word '*clothes*' is used in the previous sentence, it unfortunately means underwear. Good old hand-me-down underwear, which is a phrase that should honestly never exist in the world This specific black garbage bag of hand-me-down underwear brought forth multiple shades of Fruit of the Loom underwear in the design style commonly referred to as 'tighty-whities'. In this sense, they would technically be referred to as tighty-purples, tighty-greens, tighty-reds, and whatnot. A rainbow coloring of underwear, very pretty if you're into that sort of thing.

Several rules had been broken and lines crossed with the introduction of this black garbage bag of shame. Hand-me-down underwear is an impossibly delicate subject even within the bounds of each family's hand-me-down cycle; however, interjecting outside underwear into that delicate cycle? This is probably the biggest violation of the hand-me-down code, passing of underwear from one bloodline to another. This act is very taboo in the world of hand-me-down clothing. Mother knew this, and yet here she stood.

Number 1, the eldest of the four, and the boys' spokesman at the time, reached into the bag and pulled out a little pair of purple underwear with white seams. He squinted his eyes and cocked his head to the side as he held those purple-tighties in his hand, turning them over and over again. He was giving those tighty-purples a real thorough lookin' at, trying to figure out the best way to approach the situation. Number 2 and Number 3 flanked the left and right side of Number 1. Breathlessly they waited, arms crossed, and trying to look as intimidating as possible, letting the clothing provider know that this behavior was out of line. They spoke not a word, letting their icy glares do all the necessary communication. The fate of Number 1, Number 2, and Number 3's underwear inventory for the next half-decade hung in the balance and would be decided in the next few moments. For Number 2 and Number 3, it was like looking into the future and seeing Armageddon.

Number 1, with Number 2 and Number 3 close by his side, looked the clothing provider dead in the eye. "No" was all he said as he dropped those purple undies with the white seams back into the big black garbage bag of shame. Number 1 walked proudly away while Number 2 and Number 3 lingered for a second, arms still crossed, staring, and finally slowly shaking their heads and "tsk-ing, tsk-ing, tsk-ing" in the direction of the clothing provider.

The big bag of shame with all its colorful garments was quickly swept up by the clothing provider and whisked away. Where did it go? Who knows? Africa maybe. The Goodwill maybe. Hopefully the burn pile, never to be seen again. The provider of clothing had rolled the dice and just crapped out and she knew it. These are the dice you roll when you partake in the hand-me-down cycle—sometimes you get hot and go on a winning streak, and sometimes you crap out.

Number 1 and his staff walked away winners that day. They had drawn a clear line in the sand in regards to what clothing was acceptable for entry into the hand-me-down cycle. This was truly a victory for Number 2, and especially Number 3, whose underwear future got a little brighter that fateful day thanks to the efforts and determination of Number 1. Thanks, Number 1.

Due to the revolt, it was the last introduction of hand-me-down underwear those boys would have to endure. Yes, we had it good growing up, new underwear for everyone. Well, maybe not new undies for Number 3, but everyone else, new underwear.

THE CUSSING GAME

There are some things in life better left unsaid. Some things should be swept under the rug and remain there for all eternity. The cussing game is one of those things. The cussing game should remain unspoken, swept under that proverbial rug...but since we are here fessing up and being honest with one another, it's OK to talk about the cussing game, right? It's OK to spill the beans, yes? Then onward we proceed.

Back there in that normal house growing up, those boys were deprived of many modern-day conveniences, some of which have already been discussed and some which will be discussed later on. One of those modern-day conveniences that was absent from the normal home was an automatic dishwasher. If you were to ask the folks in charge why they didn't have a dishwasher, their response would undoubtedly be, "We don't have a dishwasher...we have four." This is a very funny joke conveying that the four boys stand in as their automatic dishwasher, very high-brow humor here.

Can you imagine the indignity of having to wash your own dishes? Historically, folks have been washing dishes by hand since Davy Crockett roamed the backwoods of Kentucky; why should the folks from the normal house be any different? We were just like the damn pioneers, only we washed our dishes without the risk of contracting typhoid or being bitten in the head by a black bear. We had it pretty good in that sense, pretty safe dishwashing conditions you could say. I guess you could go so far as to say we were living pretty high on the hog.

So there we were, playing pioneer family and washing dishes. Those dishes would be stacked as high as the eye could see. We're feeding six people here in the normal house; this is like running a small cafe. Due to the quantity of dishes, a dishwashing schedule was established by the folks in charge; when you've got yourself a labor force, you better well take advantage of it.

The schedule was set several weeks in advance so good luck getting time off of your dishwashing duties for a special occasion. "Hey it's my birthday!" "Good for you, you want to wash or rinse? We'll let you pick since it's your special day and all." That's the way it goes, now get to work and clean up that plate with the barbecued Spam residue all over it. Too bad for you if you ordered barbequed Spam or spaghetti for your special birthday meal, should've checked the dishwashing schedule before callously ordering the messiest dish ever created by man. Can you imagine the indignity? Eating like royalty for your birthday and then being thrown into the kitchen to clean it all up? Deal with it, we're hardy folks, right?

The rest of the family would carry on with their

business while the two boys assigned to do the washing and rinsing of dishes toiled away in the kitchen. Left alone to tidy up the mess that six people make when they cook and eat. Sometimes, the remaining four members of the family that were not assigned to doing hard labor in the dishwashing factory would go for walks, leaving the other two boys alone to complete the dishwashing duties.

This alone time in the dishwashing factory is where the cussing game originally reared its ugly head. The 2nd in the lineage, which is I, was coming of age, and Number 2 had discovered cussing, and cussing felt good. Cussing felt real good, and we share things that feel good, don't we? Yes, yes we do.

Before full disclosure of the cussing game is revealed, a genealogical history lesson is necessary. It's important to note that the family in the normal house has cussing in their blood. The mother of the normal house, her mother could cuss with the best of them. That is to say, the good Catholic grandma had herself a bit of a wicked tongue. Now Grandmother was a sweet old lady, and therefore she only doled out those cuss words when it was absolutely necessary, like while driving her Buick or watching Indiana University basketball. This was most certainly not in-your-face, belligerent cussing like that of a drunken English soccer hooligan—Grandmother had more respect than that. Grandmother only used her cussing talent as a last resort.

On the other side of the family lineage, the father of the normal house was a bit familiar with cussing as well. Father typically only used his cuss words when he was trying to get his point across to a stuck bolt or a faulty alternator on the big tan van. Father had inadvertently taught those boys with knobby knees a wide-array of cuss words and combinations for combining those cuss words. Like Grandmother though, these words were used as a last resort. When father's cuss words started flying in the garage, it was best to just shut your mouth and stare in the other direction, because shit was about to go down.

From both the grandmother and father, the boys in the normal house received useful, purpose-driven cussing in their genes. This was cussing that gives you that little extra nudge to get a job done or let someone know precisely how you really feel about their behavior.

The family had appropriately timed and purpose-driven cussing in their blood, real proper cussing, almost like royalty in that sense. In terms of bloodlines, the boys were getting it from both sides, so realistically, it was only a matter of time before they began dabbling on their own.

The father introduced those boys to cussing, like most fathers do, like I have now done to my kids...you're welcome, kids. But, he was in no way the master of cussing, nor am I for that matter, nor will I ever claim to be. For there is only one master...there can be only one, and he is the chosen one. In addition to the grandmother and father, the family had within its lineage, within its blood, the chosen one.

This man, the chosen one, was *The Brigadier of Bad Words*', *The King of Curse*', *The Shakespeare of Swear*'; he was, and is, a god in the cussing community, if such a community exists. If there was ever a printed publication dedicated to the art of cussing, for instance titled, *Cussing Quarterly*, the master would be on the cover every quarter, forever. The mother of that normal house has a brother, and those boys with knobby knees have an uncle, and he is the one that is called the chosen one, the master. And when that uncle cussed, the heavens parted...or cringed, depending upon who's keeping score up there. That uncle would take other people's leftover scrap-cussing and turn it into beautiful prose. That uncle showed the boys—then, and still does to this day—how cussing was meant to be done. How God, the creator of the universe, intended for cussing to be orated. The uncle is the master, and there can be no other.

The uncle's cussing was purpose-driven in the proper sense, but his cussing was also insult-laden. All of this cussing was done with a cigarette dangling from those cuss-addled lips, and an odd 'fed-up drawl' of his voice, as if to say, "I've had enough of this shit." It seemed the uncle almost enjoyed when projects went sour, just so he could pepper his fans with some classic lines of curse.

If a particular piece of machinery was breaking down and not fulfilling its particular purpose, the machinery was not called a "piece of shit", no way...talk about taking the easy way out. Uncle never took the easy way out when it came to cussing. What kind of a man do you think he is? The machinery was not called a "piece of shit", it was called a "*cock-sucking derelict whore.*" Imagine that phrase coming out of a mouth with a drawl and a Marlboro cigarette dangling from the lips. "*You derelict whore, you're a real cock-suckin' son of a bitch.*" He would often mix the beautiful curse phrases with common curse phrases, just to better connect with the common cursing man's vocabulary.

Those boys with the knobby knees would just stand and stare in awe, trying not to giggle, lest they look like amateur cussers in front of the master. What were these magical words and how did the master speak them so effortlessly and with such grace and beauty? Truly, those boys were in the presence of greatness, like Mohammed Ali in Manila.

The uncle was very deliberate and consistent with his cussing—almost every bit of prose started with or included in its opening, the phrase *'cock-sucker'*. This was almost like the uncle's way of warming up, sort of like his "ahem, may I have your attention please." However, instead of "ahem", it was "listen here cocksucker" or "welllll, aren't you just a big cock-sucker."

To avoid confusion in his cussing rants, the uncle always made it clear to whom or what he was about to bring his verbal hammer down on. If there was an issue with a back-up generator not cranking over, he would give details about that specific generator so everyone within earshot was clear on who, or what, he was referring to: "Wellllll, listen here you cocksuckin', two-cycle son of a bitch," lest we confuse this two-cycle generator with the neighbor's four-cycle generator that does not suck cock and is not a son of a bitch. The neighbor's four-cycle generator would have no doubt the uncle was not referring to it, but to the inferior two-cycle cock-sucker that lived next door.

The neighbor's four-cycle generator would say to the other appliances around him, "Hey refrigerator, you hearing this? That skinny guy smoking that Marlboro over there is really laying into that two-cycle cock-sucking generator that has the audacity to live next door to us." Such vile language from the uncle. Such appropriate language.

This historical background is vital to this particular story because it provides insight into the motives back there on those nights doing hard labor in the dishwashing factory. Those nights of hard labor when the family abandoned the washer and rinser of those stacks of dirty dishes. For when the family left, the cussing game began. There were only two objectives of the cussing game. The first was to cuss. The second was to do the first a lot. That's it. That's the point of the game...were you expecting more? I hope not, it's called the cussing game for crying out loud.

Number 2 and Number 3 were the most frequent participants in the cussing game, they were the regulars. The problem was, these two were amateur cussers. Even calling these two amateurs is probably giving them more credit than they deserve. They were woeful in the cussing arts.

If Number 2 spilled a little water while cleaning a dish, Number 3 would yell, "You dipshit Number 2, you're spilling damn water on this shitty floor." Very basic amateur cussing stuff. The boys' cuss phrases lacked creativity and purpose; it was cussing, but only by name. If those boys tried to go further into insults, it would end with mashed-up phrases such as "you stupid shit dumb head" and "ass, shit, damn, dummy-face." The mother and father of the boys would have been mortified to hear their cussing, to hear these wicked words falling from their innocent little mouths. The uncle would have been disgusted at their lack of creativity and prose, ashamed to call them his nephews, and rightfully so.

The only rule governing the cussing game was that all participants had to make sure they had cussed an equal amount of times. This was the only rule, easy enough. If the participants did not cuss equally, one participant could rat the other one out, or so went the theory. "Mom, Number 2 cussed sixty-four times and I only cussed sixty-two times, he should be in trouble." Ridiculous. What a stupid, pointless rule to govern such an important game.

The boys partaking in the game would also yell those cuss words at each other, really letting it out, if you will. Really getting into each other's faces with their cuss-laden insults. Yelling into the emptiness of the big house, those cuss words would bounce off the walls and just hang there, echoing about. They were wild with it, almost like those coach passengers in the big tan van. Cussing, frothing, wild people. Why did this happen, what end did it serve? Who knows, but it felt good to Number 2 and Number 3. It felt like freedom, and that freedom felt real good.

Looking back it's clear the cussing game's only real purpose was to let those dirty, forbidden words fly and hang there in the empty house. But, deep down inside, in their subconscious minds maybe, I think there was another reason the game was played by those naughty boys. I think that during the cussing game, those boys partaking in the game always hoped, against all odds, that one day they would piece it all together and rip off a line that would make even that old uncle of theirs take note. They imagined him hearing their beautiful cussing prose, the uncle stops and looks up from the alternator he's working on, he slowly takes a dangling Marlboro cigarette out of his mouth and stares right back at them with squinting eyes and says, "Welllll, not bad you little cock-sucker...not bad at all, nephew."

AIR CONDITIONING

Those boys with the knobby knees had no air conditioning growing up in the normal house...perish the thought. Well, save for the air conditioning provided by their holed-out reversible sweatpants, thank the lady in charge for that. For those of you keeping score at home, the list of absent modern-day conveniences was as follows: no cable television, no dishwasher, and most definitely no air conditioning. Can you imagine this life?

There were pioneers on the Oregon Trail that had it better than the folks in the normal house. When those pioneer kids on the Oregon Trail started complaining about how rough their life was on account of all the typhoid and Indians and such, those old pioneer ma's and pa's would say, "Hey, quit yer bellyachin', you could be like them poor boys in Indiana with their knobby knees and no cable TV or air conditioning."

Imagine those hot, draining, muggy, inhumane, Indiana summer days and nights. No air conditioning.

This would be borderline child abuse by today's standards, but not back then, no way. The kids nowadays have no idea. Their schools have air conditioning for heaven's sake. Schools with air conditioning. Is this ridiculous or what? Today's kids wake up in their conditioned-air homes, ride to school in their temperature-controlled car or bus, and then take their lessons...all in the comfort of 70 degrees. Never too hot, never too cold. Where's the fun in that? I implore you, where is the struggle?

Those boys in the normal house had no air conditioning, and they liked it, damn it! Only, they did not like it. They despised it with every fiber of their being. They were hardy folks, but this whole '*no air conditioning*' way of life is for the birds, as they say.

Those boys despised every warm front that came from the Gulf of Mexico. The weatherman on TV would cheerily report, "Looking forward to a warm-up towards the end of the week as the moist air from the Gulf of Mexico makes its way north." *Looking forward to?*...excuse me, who exactly is looking forward to that, Mr. Weatherman? Because here, right here in the normal house, with the mother and father and four boys with knobby knees, we sir, are not looking forward to anything that you're rambling on about.

There was of course one exception to this. There was one individual of the normal house that *was* looking forward to that warm-up coming at the end of the week; it was the father figure, the big man in charge. He liked the heat—"prefer the heat" he would say. The man would sleep in a sauna if they'd let him, whoever 'they' is. He would never admit it, but I think he liked to watch his Labor Force sweat it out at night, building character one miserable, sweaty night after the next.

The nights were the absolute worst for those dear little boys. Stifling, dead air hanging in the bedrooms, like the Grim Reaper himself was breathing his hot, fiery breath on those boys.

Maybe a few fans could help the situation? Get that dead air moving? Maybe even create a nice little wind tunnel for moving air, move that hot air out of those stifling bedrooms? Well, therein lies the next problem. The normal house had in its possession three bedrooms, therefore the family possessed three fans—no more, no less. For those not good at arithmetic that's a ratio of one fan for every bedroom.

It seems perhaps that in the difficult economic climate of the late 1980s the fan industry had gone belly-up, right alongside with the Free Rock Store. No more fans coming off the production lines. Sorry Earthlings, everyone is going to have to just live with the fans they've got from here on out. Hopefully none of those fans break or we're royally screwed, because the world is fresh out of new fans, and there's no plans to build any more.

So there they were, with their three bedrooms and three fans. Again, that's a one-to-one fan-to-bedroom ratio, not good. This fan ratio was not enough fan power to move the air, let alone enough movement to even think about starting a breezy wind tunnel. One fan per room was just enough to bring more outside hot air into the room. Stuff those rooms with all the hot air you could find. Folks from the hot air balloon industry were becoming jealous of all the hot air those bedrooms had. Those hot air balloon folks would call the family, asking about maybe purchasing some of that hot air, but the family wasn't in the business of selling hot air. No, the family was in the 'dying of heat exhaustion' business...and business was booming. Was the family fan-rich? Not so much.

The neighbors would talk in hushed tones during the summer months: "There go those folks from the normal house, I've heard they only have three fans...tsk, those poor poor boys, what with their knobby knees and sweaty little mullet-covered heads." It was rough. It was the dark times. Things were looking pretty shabby around those times.

During those hot summer months, the complaints would come down from those young boys as soon as the lights went out for bedtime. "We're too hot to sleep, our skin is melting off," and so on and so forth. It was possible the boys were slightly embellishing the degree of their suffering; they had been known to do that from time to time. The standard response from management was, and probably still would be to this day: "Stop moving and it won't feel so hot." I know for a fact that this would still be the response. I am a father now and have uttered equally ridiculous responses to my children, trying to pacify them for just a moment or two of silence.

"Stop moving," those management folks would say. Just stop moving?!...hmm, interesting idea. We've never thought of just 'not moving', well that's easy enough. See, we've been doing this going-to-sleep-in-the-sweltering-Amazon-rainforest-like-room thing wrong this whole time. We've been lying in bed and thrashing all about, doing sit-ups and push-ups up here in the old sweat-box, trying to cool ourselves down that way. Here, all along it turns out it was best to just stop moving...well that's easy. Easy peasy in fact. So easy we can do it in our sleep, if only that sweet release would come. "Thanks for the advice, oh wise ones."

Stop moving and maybe the Lord Jesus will grace you with the finality of passing out from heat exhaustion. Maybe he would, maybe he wouldn't, but most likely he wouldn't. Only time would tell. Jesus had neither the time nor the energy, quite frankly, to help four whiny boys with knobby knees reach their slumber. Jesus would look down and say, "Christ, just stop moving so much and you'll fall asleep." Thanks, Jesus.

Yes sir, times were tough at the normal house in the dead of summer, when the Gulf of Mexico would send us her putrid air.

With the installation of air conditioning nowhere even close to being on the list of possibilities for the foreseeable future, the boys with the sweaty little heads were left with no other option but to create their own air conditioning. Sounds like a great idea, how hard could it be? Somebody should've thought of this a long time ago.

The ideas for these homemade air conditioning units were bad and the execution of the ideas was even worse; mostly because those boys were just kids and had no real world idea about how refrigeration actually worked, When thinking of these ideas, the word 'pathetic' quickly comes to mind. Thank the Lord Jesus that most of the ideas themselves are now lost to the annals of time, lest they be embarrassingly revisited here in these ramblings.

One particularly poorly planned idea was not lost to the annals of time, however. This idea survived the test of time, perhaps because it was the worst idea for homemade air conditioning ever created. The premise for this air conditioning idea was fairly rudimentary as you can imagine. First, you obtain one large mixing bowl. Second, raid the family freezer and empty all the ice cubes from the trays into said mixing bowl, filling it to the brim with ice. Third, close all the doors and windows in the bedroom you are trying to cool. Last, turn the one allotted bedroom fan on high and point it towards the bowl of ice. (Just writing this paragraph now fills the author with dread for how ridiculously stupid and pathetic this idea sounds.) The final contraption was as follows: one mixing bowl filled with 15 pathetically small ice cubes being blown on by one fan, a fan that has the blowing capacity of a 95-year-old chain-smoking grandmother with emphysema. How could this not work, how could this not cool that bedroom?

In order to get the maximum cooling efficiency, the bowl that the ice was placed into needed to be tilted downward so the air from the fan could hit it at the right angle to produce the desired frigid air. With more surface area of the ice exposed to the quick-moving air, it was easy to see how the desired results would transpire. This is simple physics really, if you don't understand these simple principles of thermodynamics then honestly I feel bad for you. Now then, one freezing-cold room coming right up.

The boys that created this air conditioner wanted to be surprised by the efficiency of their contraption, so after setting it up, they closed the door and left the room. After anxiously waiting an hour, the door to the now ice-cold room was to be opened, the moment of truth was upon them. Before opening the door, they placed their hand against it, this was to make sure the room wasn't too cold to enter. The hand to the door provided the boys with puzzling results as the bedroom door was still warm...hmmm...this was an odd and unexpected result for the boys about to enter the ice box. The boys chalked this odd occurrence up to the fact that the doors were very well insulated and were doing their job in keeping that frigid air in. A job well done, door. This was very good thinking on the part of the constructor of the house, make these rooms airtight.

Upon finally entering the room, the boys discovered that the room was not cold, or colder, or coldest, or any other iteration of the word 'cold' that might imply something was un-warm. No, the room was now actually hotter than before. This was on account of having all that hot air trapped in there with no windows or door for it to escape. The ice that was supposed to provide the refrigerant in the bowl had turned to water, and due to the fact that the boys had tilted the bowl for maximum airflow, the now melted water had spilled all over the carpet. This is simple physics really, and if you don't understand that then I feel bad for you.

The end result of their personal air conditioning unit was a warmer room and soggy carpet. Defeat. Absolute, 100% crushing defeat. Back to the old drawing board...only there was no drawing board, it had melted.

This ice bowl air conditioning fiasco set the boys' homemade air conditioning industry into a tailspin. It seemed the bowl of ice was the best idea those sweaty little brains could come up with. When that idea failed, they folded up shop and called it quits. Suck it up and deal with it. Helpful hint: it's been rumored that if you just lie still then it's not so bad, simple really.

But air conditioning would one day come to the normal house. Years and years later after the failed homemade air conditioning units, real air conditioning would come. Oh, would it come, in all its cooling-air glory.

A member of the normal house's extended family happened to be throwing away an old busted-up window air conditioning unit. What's that you say? Throwing away? Simply tossing into the trash to go live with all those bad, ugly rocks that had been tossed aside? Well excuse me Mr. 'I'm-so-rich-I-throw-air-conditioners-away', don't send that horse to pasture quite yet. Don't go throwing that big box of cooling possibilities into the landfill. Number 2, which is I, begged and pleaded with the folks in charge to acquire the piece-of-junk air conditioner for his place of slumber.

Through tense hours of negotiating and mediating, an agreement was finally reached between Number 2 and the management folks of the normal house. Number 2 agreed to pay the increased cost in utilities that this old junker would no doubt cause, and the air conditioner could be installed. Deal! Hallelujah! Jesus was finally listening. Prayers had been answered, the gods smiled down. Number 2 signed on to this deal knowing full well no payment would ever be expected for the increased price of the utility bill. Some deals were just like that in the normal house. Both parties would agree to a deal knowing full well it wouldn't amount to diddly squat. This was one of those deals, best kind of deals around for getting free air conditioners.

As for the air conditioner? It was old, really old. This air conditioner was so old it seemed to pre-date electricity, if that's even possible. Benjamin Franklin had created this air conditioner and then realized he hadn't even flown his kite in the thunderstorm to come up with the idea for inventing electricity yet; that's how old this thing was

The Benjamin Franklin air conditioner was huge. It was a behemoth. It barely even fit into the window of the bedroom it was meant to cool. To top it off, this hulking, old air conditioner was loud, boy was it loud. Unspeakably loud. Like, Boeing 747 taking off in your bedroom kind of loud. This thing was cranking out some real decibels. That old air conditioner was loud when it turned on, it was loud when it conditioned the air, and it most certainly was loud when it turned off. It was a loud-ass 4-ton air conditionin' cock-suckin' son-of-a-bitch, as the cussing uncle would've orated. But, boy oh boy, did it cool the bedroom. So cool, so nice.

That old piece of junk cooled the room a million times better than some old mixing bowl with ice cubes crammed into it. That old air conditioner made quick work of the small bedroom it was tasked with cooling; easiest job it ever had. This was like a retirement home for the air conditioner. Someplace the old air conditioner could just go to live out the rest of its days doing easy work, keeping this one sweaty boy here nice and cool.

Lord alive though, did that air conditioner shake the house when it turned on and off. When that old air conditioner kicked on, everyone in the neighborhood knew the cold air was flowing. It would shake the whole house, night and day, always shaking. The air conditioner excelled at three things and three things only, and it did those three things in this specific order: 1. Being loud. 2. Shaking the house 3. Cooling the air.

Of course this loud, shaking behemoth of metal bothered everyone in the house, except Number 2. Number 2 would wake up to the shaking and groggily smile...grab a handful of blanket and pull it up over his ears..."sure is cold in here," he would say, as he drifted back to dreams of penguins and polar bears dancing through shaking earthquakes. These were the good times for Number 2, sleeping in the cold, conditioned, shaking room. Yes sir, things were alright back then.

THE CODE OF SILENCE

Summertime meant time spent at the lake house. And boy did those boys have it good at the lake house. No air conditioning needed there, folks. What with the nice cool breezes delivered fresh from the lake nightly. Warm front moving in? Bring it on, we're at the lake now, that Gulf of Mexico air can do us no harm up here. The family would load that big tan van to the gills and hit the road come summertime. Those folks back in coach would toss some baby carrots out the windows and poof!...here we are at the lake. Times were good, yes sir.

At the lake, even the normal day-to-day rules seemed to take a vacation. "Folks in charge, can we stay up late tonight...like...super late?" "Stay up late? Sure...we're at the lake, who cares, man? Have yourself a few Faygo soda pops while you're staying up late, man." Apparently, the folks in charge became so relaxed at the lake house they starting referring to the boys as '*man*'.

Generally speaking, those boys had it pretty good

at the lake house. Partly because the lake relaxes everyone, and partly because all the folks in management drank a bit of hooch when they were at the lake, helping them to relax even further. Nothing on this here blue planet helps kids get away with a bit more than when parents have a buzz on account of the booze. I've experienced this now, I know it to be true. Don't want to brush your teeth before bed? Don't care. Want to brush your teeth with Oreos as toothpaste? Don't care. Don't even want to go to bed? Honestly, I couldn't care less; grab me a beer from the fridge and you can watch *The Exorcist* while drinking cherry Kool-Aid and eating cheese puffs on the white couch for all I care. This is how it happens, it's how it all goes down when parents get a bit of hooch in them. The lake was definitely no exception to this and only amplified those feelings.

Supervision rules even became more relaxed while at the lake house, mostly because the folks in management wanted a break from all the chaos of those four boys with knobby knees. So those folks in charge would go on boat rides all by their lonesome. "Leave them boys at home," they'd say. Toss the house keys to old Number 1 and say, "See ya later, chump." And these weren't speeding around the lake variety boat rides...these were cruising, not a care in the world, type boat rides. These were, 'pack a cooler baby, we're hittin' the water and won't be back for a few hours' type of boat rides. These were pre-children type of boat rides—no worries, no responsibilities.

So off those management folks would go, off into the big open expanse of the lake. And the boys? Those precious boys with knobby knees and sweatpants with holes in the back? Those boys stayed home, or technically, at the lake house. A little time on their own, so to speak. It should come as no surprise to anyone that the boys preferred this arrangement. It was a silent agreement that the two sides had entered into; the two sides being the folks in management and the boys with knobby knees. No one is really sure when the agreement was made, but make no mistake, it was firmly in place.

The agreement was there, governing the rules of boat-ride etiquette. Management was always very polite about these unspoken rules, and this was not lost on the boys. The management folks would cordially invite those boys to come along for a ride, secretly praying those boys would say no. The boys of course would politely decline. Prayers answered, thanks big-bearded man from heaven. Sometimes, older folks, folks in management, need some time away from the folks they are supervising. I understood that then, I fully understand that now. So off they go, you kids stay here and watch over the place. Don't get yourselves into any trouble...or at least any trouble that requires a member of the medical profession, police, or protection services to arrive on the scene.

With the management folks gone, those boys had some free time on their hands. As the saying goes, *when the cat's away, the mice will play*...and by play, they mean get into trouble or break rules. Not strong armed robbery sort of trouble, nothing that would get anyone sent to the big house. Just enough rule-breaking to make it feel like you're living a little.

The thing with those boys with knobby knees though, was they also had a code of silence to govern their rule-breaking. And their code of silence was a damn good code...almost airtight in fact.

Any trouble between the boys, any fights or beatings that occurred while the folks were away on their boat rides, those fights stayed strictly confidential and any hard feelings ended the moment the management folks got back. Why, you might ask? Why would those boys not rat one another out? Make a scene and such, get each other in trouble? The reason is simple: if those folks in management know what's going down when they're gone, then the jig is up, it's all over man. Kiss your little slice of freedom goodbye. Pack that cooler full of apple juice, because now we're all going on that long boat ride, and there is nobody happy with this arrangement. And guess what, kiddos? There's no windows to throw baby carrots out of on the boat like there is the big tan van. No highway to watch those baby carrots go boing boing boing down the road. On the boat ride, carrots thrown overboard would just float away, and let's be honest here, there's nothing really very funny about a floating carrot. I mean, it's a little bit funny, but not boinging down the highway kind of funny. No sir, there's none of that boinging-carrot fun to be had out there on the boat rides, out on the open water. It was in everyone's best interest to keep their damn lips shut about any trouble that occurred. "Loose lips lead to boat rides," as they said back when the world was at war with itself.

Now most of the mischief that the boys got into while the management folks were away amounted to a hill of beans, which is to say, it was nothing really too major. No harm, no foul sort of stuff. It involved a lot of playing cops and robbers with fake guns and drinking Faygo soda until they felt the need to puke brought on by an acute case of sugar-belly. Those boys were typically only allowed one soda per day, but when there ain't no boss, there ain't no rules. So grab yourself a Faygo Red Pop and slug that baby down. Thirsty for another? Grab another, who cares?!? Drink it up, live it up, we've got two hours until the folks in management are back on the scene. How many grape sodas can you plug through in 120 minutes?

Now oftentimes, the mischief the boys found would turn into picking on someone, and by someone, that means Number 4. This is what brothers do. Always have, always will. It wasn't intentional and it never started out with the intent to go after Number 4, but just like shit rolling downhill, it always has to stop somewhere, and it usually stops at the bottom. And at the bottom was Number 4.

Number 4 was different than the other three boys though, he was cut from a different cloth so to speak. To be perfectly blunt, Number 4 was tough. Tough as a damn ox. Way tougher than those other three boys. Number 4 didn't take no shit from nobody, least of all his three older brothers. Those other boys would try to break Number 4, but as they would come to find out, he was unbreakable. Number 4 always fought back and it came to be discovered that apparently he was not born with the gene to know how, or when, to back down. Three against one? Number 4 does not care. Absolutely couldn't care less. Probably preferred it that way actually, bring it on. Those other boys could contain Number 4 but not for long—he always found a way out, and when he did, the shit would really hit the fan.

One fateful day, while the management folks

lounged on a pleasure cruise around that big old body of water, World War III was breaking out at the lake house. Like most wars that happen on planet earth, this war did not start with a big offensive. There was no 'shock and awe' campaign to kick this war off. This war started as a simmer, it slowly simmered until it boiled, and then it boiled over and war broke out.

The third world war was not started by Number 4, but it was most definitely a war ended by Number 4. Those other three boys had roughed him up good. The roughing up which started playful, as it always did, ended in a wedgie to end all wedgies. For those unversed on the topic, a wedgie is the pulling of one's underwear up from the rear as far as it will go. This is a very uncomfortable feeling to the recipient of the wedgie. The wedgie the three boys inflicted on Number 4 was a wedgie that would make any man wish he had been born a woman. What started with giggling and laughing ended with a primal scream coming from the bowels of Number 4. As legend has it, some folks say if you're real quiet, if you're real still...you can still hear the scream echoing in the woods behind the lake house to this very day...the scream that started World War III.

Those three boys that had inflicted the wedgie knew the moment that primal scream went out that the fun time was over. They knew they had gone too far. Hit the road boys, the shit has officially hit the fan. And hit the road they did. They skedaddled, for they had unleashed hell, and hell was pissed.

Number 4, in his wedgie-fueled anger, located the largest weapon he could find. The weapon of choice was a huge plastic yellow paddle. Those boys' sweet, sweet grandmother had bought her little grandbabies these yellow paddles as part of some outdoor tennis-like game. Those sweet grandbabies that were so sweet they wouldn't hurt a fly.

This yellow plastic paddle was not soft, pliable, won't-hurt-you-much-if-you-get-hit type of plastic. Lord no. It was the opposite of that. This was some real sturdy yellow plastic. This was plastic of the type that NASA had decided was too sturdy to be employed on their space shuttles and rockets. The grandmother had originally tried to sell the plastic yellow paddles to NASA, thinking they might be of some use to the space agency. However, NASA was afraid that if they tried to land a spaceship made of this yellow plastic on the lunar surface, it would possibly dent the moon. Instead they marketed these big yellow plastic paddles to kids as some cockameemee tennis-like game.

This yellow plastic paddle was a big yellow paddle of retribution, and Number 4 was swinging it like a wildman possessed...mostly because he was a wildman possessed. This was Number 4's moment, this was his Revolutionary War. Three against one. Bring. It. On.

He chased his prey, those three skinny older boys—Numbers 1, 2, and 3, all around the house and yard The three boys being chased screamed and squealed for their lives. They screamed like it was the end of days. Screamed with their little girly-sounding screams. And they ran, oh boy did they run. They ran for their little pathetic lives. For this was judgment day, and Number 4 was handing down the judgments.

After running wildly around the lake house, the wildman finally cornered his prey, with his big yellow paddle by his side. Numbers 1, 2, and 3 had taken refuge in the family boat house; holed up if you will.

This boat house did not store boats though, it mostly just stored all the family's lake stuff—water toys, life-jackets, and such. The lake house was built on a hill, and built into this hill was the boathouse. Therefore one could walk onto the roof of the boat house, it was a concrete slab in fact. The following picture displays the holding cell for Numbers 1, 2, and 3 during World War III. The tactical advantage for Number 4 can easily be seen.

The family typically used this concrete slab as a deck, for lounging and such. Number 4 was now using the roof of the boathouse as his guard post. So there sat the wildman, Number 4, waiting, stalking his prey as those three scared little ones cowered below him in the boat house. Waiting, hoping, praying that the folks in management would for some reason cut their long leisurely boat ride short.

But management did not cut their boat ride short,

management was completely oblivious to the world war occurring at the lake house. The folks from management were out there on the open water having the time of their lives, cruising and pretending they were free again.

The three boys in the boat house could hear the wildman above them...stalking them like a lion stalks a gazelle. The wildman was waiting for one of those three boys to muster up the courage to make a move. He was hitting his big yellow paddle on the concrete slab, muttering some language only the devil himself could understand. Number 4 felt no need to come down and confront those three cornered kittens with a frontal assault; he had them right where he wanted them. He was smug in this. He relished in it, as he should, standing guard over his captives.

After many minutes of this banging and muttering, there was a sudden silence. The pounding, the muttering, it all ceased...radio silence. Those three little scared kittens wondered what was going on up there. Should those three boys peek out? Have a looksee, try and catch a glimpse of the wildman? No. Only a crazy person would tempt the wildman at a time like this. And Numbers 1, 2, and 3 were not crazy, they were just scared silly. There was only one thing to do at this point, and that was to wait it out.

Numbers 1, 2, and 3 sat and waited. They waited for minutes with no sound, they waited for hours...weeks it seemed had passed and there was still nothing, no sound. Surely the wildman had left by now. Did they peek their heads out to see if he was still there? See if the wildman was still guarding his prey? God no. Those three boys did the next logical thing: they sat down there in the dank, musty boathouse and drank Faygo sodas.

The boat house also doubled as the keeper of the family's auxiliary refrigerator...the old 'beer and pop fridge' as people call them. So those boys drank their Faygo sodas like they were their final death row meals...making toasts, saying thanks to one another, and "what a wonderful life we have lived, I am honored to die here, with two of my brothers, at the hands of the wildman, Number 4."

Those three boys had brought it upon themselves and so there they sat—'*if you can't do the time, then don't do the crime*', as they say in the prison business. Numbers 1, 2, and 3 had done the crime and now they were doing the time. Fair is fair, no way around that, it is what it is. And so there they sat, doing hard time, slugging down a few last Faygo sodas before heading on up to the pearly gates to meet old Saint Pete and the bearded big man himself.

After what seemed to be five weeks of waiting, that slow boat from China finally appeared on the horizon carrying those happy folks from management. The folks from management were back and the shit was really going to hit the fan this time. Those three little kittens emerged slowly from their cell, waiting for the big yellow paddle of death to rain down upon them from above.

But rain down from above it did not. Nor did the proverbial fan get hit by any poop. Number 4 was gone, he had left weeks ago in fact. He'd lost interest in his duties as jail keeper and simply walked off the job, he'd had enough. The captive three emerged and waited for their punishment. But punishment never came. Number 4, the wildman, true to the code of silence, remained steadfast. Number 4 understood that no punishment from management could achieve what he had accomplished with a primal scream and a big yellow paddle of death. Number 4 was feared now, he had respect, street cred. Number 4 was no longer a subject to be messed with while the cats were away on their pleasure cruises; he knew that, and so did the other boys

Due to the enforcement of the Code of Silence, there was no lingering evidence from the confrontation, save for one thing; the big yellow paddle. Every once in a while the wildman, Number 4, would pull that yellow paddle out of its special hiding spot. He would pick it up and feel the power in his hands as he stared at those other three boys. Give a good old wildman stare to Numbers 1, 2, and 3. Sending the message, "Remember this, fellas? Remember my yellow paddle? Remember that day?" And Number 1, Number 2, and Number 3...they all remembered it. They remembered real, real good.

As mentioned at the beginning of the chapter, the code of silence was pretty airtight, but it was not completely airtight. The code of silence was broken once, and only once by those boys. On a separate occasion, while those folks from management were out cruising the lake, another fight was breaking out at the homestead. It was a fight with no real beginning but a very definitive ending.

A gym shoe was thrown, a glass window in a door was broken. Fight over. Hey, shit, have you met my friend, fan? Good luck covering that one up, boys. No code of silence can sweep a broken window under the rug. Can't exactly get the tape out and mend that window back to health, back to its previous state of wholeness. No sir, the window was broken and there was going to be hell to pay.

And here's the real skinny about the code of silence, the real funny thing. Once the code of silence was breached, all bets were off. Once one of those brothers crosses the line and mentions a name during interrogation, the code is squashed, poof...gone, like a piece of broccoli on the highway at 55 mph. Accusations were thrown around, names were given out, every man for himself type of stuff. Everyone was getting thrown under the bus now that the code had been breached.

Alibis were floated, but the folks in management were in no mood to hear any of them out. Who threw the shoe? Doesn't matter that it was Number 3. Who provoked the thrower? It honestly does not matter that Number 1 was roughing Number 3 up. Was Number 2 minding his own damn business and just tidying up the lake house while trying to get a nice spaghetti dinner on the table for the family to share? Doesn't matter, why didn't he step in to stop the fight? Was Number 4 combing his mullet and practicing *wildman* smiles with his big yellow paddle in the mirror? Probably, but that's irrelevant at this point. Everyone was going down for this one, all four of them. And down they went. Every last one of those boys was in trouble, rank and file.

Allowances were confiscated and mandatory boat rides were had. The jig was most definitely up. Pack the coolers with apple juice, fellas, time to start going for boat rides. Lessons were learned and the lesson was this: don't throw shoes at windows. You understand that lesson, Number 3?

SWIMMING POOL

As mentioned in earlier ramblings, the folks of the mother of the normal house had in their possession a swimming pool. Those boys with knobby knees had grandparents that had a swimming pool, and with that, life was real good. This swimming pool was of the above-ground variety, and it was smack dab in the middle of the city. A little oasis of water in the hustle and bustle of city life, if you will.

Now swimming pools in and of themselves present many problems and maintenance nightmares. None of which really befront the lives of little kids, who couldn't actually care less about the hassle of owning one of these damn little bodies of water. What's the pH level of the water? How much chlorine should we add? C'mon, really? Kids don't care about that shit, let's just get to the swimming part already, that's where the fun is!

However, kids do understand the biggest drag about owning a pool. It is universally agreed upon, by adults and kids alike, that the worst part about owning a pool is the time it takes filling the thing up. It takes hours...days...weeks it seems. Half the swimming season is gone by the time you get the damn things filled with all that water. Unless of course you can find a better way. Which, by the way, there is always a better way of doing things.

Of course, to find that better way of doing things it's usually necessary to give a few of the elder statesmen of the family a few frosty Old Milwaukee Lights, Hamms, or Pabst Blue Ribbon cans of beer and a little bit of time. Those elder statesmen, after getting a few brews in them, can let their minds relax a little bit and then come up with a better, more workable solution. It just so happened there were several members of the family that liked to drink those frosty Old Milwaukee Lights and Pabst Blue Ribbons and conjure up these "better plans".

The above picture shows clear evidence of one such session where the elder statesmen are deeply involved in concocting a better plan. (Cutoff jean shorts and mustaches apparently were very "in" at the time.)

After a few rounds of those beers, the conversations would finally get around to the topic of filling the pool: "Say...isn't Uncle So-and-So a firefighter?" "Why yes, yes I do believe he is, why do you ask?" "Well, I was thinking see, don't firefighters have really good methods for delivering large quantities of water in an expedited manner?" "Why yes...yes they do, they're called firehoses." "You know...that firefighting uncle is sitting right next to you drinking an Old Milwaukee Light, why don't you ask him these things?" "Good thinking." And so it went; real high-level type of conversations.

As luck would have it, a member of the family was in the city fire department, as the previous paraphrased conversation so accurately outlined. In case you are unaware, fire departments have access to very large quantities of water...fast-moving, large quantities of water. Well there's your solution boys, hook those fire hoses to the city fire hydrants to fill up the swimming pool. Reduce those hours of boredom and waiting while you fill up the pool to mere minutes. Problem solved; get your swimming suits on, kiddos.

While we're on the topic of filling things up, we could fill up a million rinsed-out milk jugs to load in the big tan van so we don't have to shit in metal pots in the dead of winter, yes? No, we cannot. This would just be taking advantage of the firefighting uncle's status within the city fire department and we shouldn't dare do that, it's not good form. What kind of people do you think we are? Grifters?

So those elder statesmen decided the proper thing to do was to use the city fire hydrants for filling the swimming pool; why else would the city put the hydrant there if they didn't want it to be used? The city was so nice to provide a water source like that, very courteous of them. So, they blasted that pool full of water, what a novel idea.

Only, there's a slight problem. Like any idea formed while drinking Old Milwaukee Lights, there's always a problem, a little catch, if you will. The opening of a fire hydrant usually leads to iron and rust breaking loose in the water lines that are buried below the city streets; this is not good. In fact, it is very not good. It is the opposite of good, it is bad. All that water that has been sitting there stagnant for the last year begins to experience precipitation of the commonly found metal in water—iron. This precipitation is due to certain chemical reactions which will not be explored in this space, but this is simple chemistry really, look it up.

Once those water lines are opened, and that iron sediment gets all excited and rustled up, it comes along for the ride with all that water. That wonderful swimming pool that was filled in five minutes with a blasting city fire department hose? It was filled with rust-colored water. Anybody up for a swim? No thanks, going to take a big pass on that. So now they've got to empty the pool and fill it up again, repeat the whole dang process. No big deal, right? Everyone just remain calm, open up a new round of brewskis and just hook that big ol' firehose up to the fire hydrant, and fire it up again.

After the elder statesmen had done this once, twice, or maybe three times, the neighbors started picking up on what's going down over there. All that iron and rust that's getting rustled up, it starts paying a visit to the neighbors' sinks, to their toilets, and especially to their white clothes that are being washed in their washing machines. Those neighbors start noticing their water is now orange, and are those neighbors happy about this development? Are those friendly little neighbors tickled pink? Their white clothing has been turned pink, but they themselves are not tickled pink. They are quite un-pleased to be perfectly blunt. Those neighbors are so un-pleased they make a special phone call to the city police department and have the whole swimming pool operation shut down. Pretty rude behavior if you ask me.

With the swimming pool operation shut down, where does that leave the folks with the empty pool? It leaves them filling the damn pool like every other family, with a tiny garden hose and a lot of time, and honestly there's absolutely no fun in that method. What's the point of having a fireman in the family if he can't be properly utilized? It takes a lot of the fun out of things, I can tell you that much. So there they were, filling their above-ground pool like every other schmuck, with the old green garden house, one measly drop at a time.

Finally, after 300 hours of drip, drip, drip from the garden hose, they've got themselves a pool full of clean water and swimming time had arrived. Only thing is, those boys with knobby knees are small. Small boys, and small girls for that matter, are not typically known for their swimming abilities. The solution to this little problem is easy and very straightforward: life jackets; jackets that save your life. As with the seatbelts in the station wagon and big tan van, the idea of safety had not fully arrived on the scene at the time. Being the 1980s, safety was still in its wild west phase where pretty much anything goes. Being safe was unfashionable at the time, it seemed. Today's life jackets are not the life jackets of yesteryear. Not. Even. Close.

In the previous paragraph, when the word '*life jacket*' was used, the correct description for what was actually used in the family swimming pool would be 'foam footballs of death'. The foam footballs of death were exactly as they sound. These life jackets were foam, shaped into the form of a football. This foam football was to be secured to the back of the little ones to keep them afloat. So there those boys were, trying to learn to swim with foam footballs strapped to their backs.

The foam only had one care in the world: the foam football life jacket was out for itself. The foam football was an egotistical bastard if ever there was one. The foam wanted to float and survive, and anything attached to it needed to be underneath it, maybe help its buoyancy a bit. The foam football was kind of a jerk in this manner, real snooty.

For the children blessed with wearing the foam footballs of death, this meant a furious doggie-paddle was necessary to stay afloat...paddle paddle paddle, little one. Keep those bony little pony legs furiously kicking. Paddle like your little life depends on it...because it does in fact depend on it.

In the following photo a child can be seen struggling to stay afloat while the foam football does its best to punish the child for trying to have an enjoyable time swimming. The terror can clearly be seen on the child's face as he reaches for the ladder while struggling with every kick. Will he reach the ladder before the foam football pushes him under?

As if the egotistical foam footballs were not bad enough in and of themselves, they also featured a metal clasp that went across the belly to hold the foam ball secure in its place. The chance that this metal clasp caught little kid belly skin when it was strapped to those little bodies was 100%. It happened every time and there was no getting around it. Deal with it, kid. If you want to go swimming there's going to be a little bit of pain involved and a whole lot of paddling for your little life.

These foam footballs of death, while evil, were actually good for several things. First, they separated out the weak from the strong. Old Chuck Darwin would most assuredly have approved of these life jackets on account of his Theory of Evolution and its premise of the strongest surviving. If you couldn't handle the foam football, down you went, underneath the water as the football floated over you, waiting for a parents' hand to grab you and out of the pool you came. Maybe wait until next year, kid, until you are ready to face the full strength of the foam football. The second thing the foam footballs of death were good for was those boys were forced to swim and you better learn pretty damn fast. Mission accomplished, foam footballs...mission accomplished.

Even with the foam footballs of death, the pool was good. The pool was better than good, actually, it was great. Most kids don't have access to a lake house let alone a pool, especially a pool in the middle of the big city. Yet, here we were, with access to both. Yes sir, times were good, we were living high on the hog. Swimming at the lake, swimming in the big city, this was as good as it gets.

The times were good. But, the times were only good until they weren't good. The times became un-good one year late in the swimming season. That swimming pool, that poor above-ground swimming pool that had been blasted with a firehouse more times than it could count, that swimming pool that had served as a lounging spot for the family for years, that pool that had taught those boys with knobby knees to swim by strapping big foam footballs to their backs, that old pool was getting tired. Real tired, in fact. Tired like it had just spent a day gathering rocks, that kind of tired.

That old swimming pool was getting up there in the years as they say. And today, this very day right here, that old swimming pool just can't hold it together anymore. When swimming pools can't hold it together anymore, there's no talking them out of it. There's no talking them off the ledge, as they say in the anti-suicide business.

Once those swimming pools reach their decision that it's all done for, that decision is set in stone. It's like trying to win an argument with Number 4 in the lineage, good luck with that. Decision made, move on. So that old swimming pool woke up one fateful day and said, "I've had enough of this shit, I'm ready to head on up to the big swimming pool in the sky...I. Am. Done." And done it was.

One side of that swimming pool opened up, opened up for the whole world to see. The swimming pool had several options on where she should dump her motherload of chlorinated water. That is to say, that where the pool was situated it was almost universally surrounded by grass and earth. In fact, the majority of area moving away from the swimming pool was surrounded by plain old water-absorbing dirt and grass, no harm there. The earth will gladly accept that water.

Other than all that grass and soil, there was a small sliver of land on one side of the pool that was a driveway, which fed into a city alley. A narrow, high-walled, concrete, big-city alley. Now most swimming pools are nice and polite, and when those nice, polite pools decide that their time has come, they do the polite thing and dump their contents on the yard. Nice. Polite. Real swell fella that pool was, dumping all that water on this here lawn. Grandmother and Grandfather's pool was not nice. It was not polite. It was tired, old, and apparently mad at the world. This swimming pool wanted to go out with a bang, and so it did. This swimming pool picked the one spot that would maximize casualties when she opened up; the alley. The alley side of that old pool opened up, unleashing one million gallons of water down that canyon that up until this point in time had served as a big-city concrete alley. Now we've got ourselves a big-city canyon with its very own river flowing through it; very cosmopolitan.

In that newly created river now rushing through the city streets, the neighbor's dog was swept away. That neighbor's dog was just wandering around, minding its own business, doing doggy things in the alley, and the next thing he knew, a torrent of water was upon him. Now listen closely, there are many things in these pages and ramblings that are partly, or completely embellished, but rest assured, this is not one of those embellishments. The neighbor's dog was swept away. Poof. Gone. Like broccoli on the highway at 55 mph.

That dog got a taste of some good old-fashioned class-five rapids right there in the big city. See you later puppy, hope your little doggie paws can strap a foam football of death onto your little doggie back before you get too far down the river. Hope you don't get any of your fur caught on the metal clasp that goes across your little doggy belly. The doggy was gone and who knows if it's ever coming back. No need for the neighbors to call the police on this little misadventure, because there's jack-shit they can do about it

As a side note, this is the quickest way to drain a pool. Whoosh! Gone. And with all that water that swept away, all those hours of lounging in the pool, of learning to swim, of grade-A relaxation right there in the big city...those good times were all swept away as well, down the city streets with the neighbor's dog. Poof. Gone.

After the pool-letting, the remaining shell of that mean, spiteful swimming pool was removed from the property. There's no going back after a pool-letting of that magnitude. No amount of Bond-O or glue or tape is fixing that gaping hole in the side of the old heap that once was a swimming pool. Scrap the whole damn thing, send it to the landfill to die and rot.

In the place of the swimming pool? Grass. Boring, non-swimmable, stupid green grass. It was all over. We were back to being second-class citizens. Only able to swim at our lake house, which was eight hours away and with no baby carrots for the drive. Times were rough back then, that's for sure. These were like the dark ages.

BIRDS

The father of the normal house had a mother that loved birds. That is to say, the boys with knobby knees had a grandmother that loved birds. The word *'loved'* is sorely misrepresenting the depth of appreciation the grandmother had for all things feathered. When Grandmother put up her Christmas tree to celebrate the birth of the Lord and savior Jesus Christ, the majority of the ornaments were bird related. Bird ornaments that apparently were created when a taxidermist had shrunk down some real life birds and put some flexible wiring on their feet to wrap around Christmas tree branches. The taxidermist had then sold those little birds as ornaments...and Grandmother had bought the lot of them; put the bird ornament salesmen right out of business in fact. Those grandchildren of course loved the bird ornaments, what a novel idea, what a great Christmas tree. Ornaments that you can actually play with. Grandmother was ahead of her time in that respect.

The grandmother's love for birds cannot be understated. She watched birds outside, she had books about birds, she even took up painting so that she could paint birds on canvas. Birds, birds, and more birds. Couldn't get enough of the damn birds. If you were to ask Grandmother which animal she would prefer to be if she had the chance to be reincarnated as an animal, her answer would most definitely would be a bird. Any bird in particular, Grandmother? Doesn't matter what bird, any old bird would do. Grandmother even had a sister that everyone called Birdie—you can't make this stuff up. Birds ran deep in that family; all the way to the core.

This grandmother was adored by those boys, as most grandmothers are. Those boys can do no wrong in her eyes, and she can do no wrong in theirs; pretty standard grandmother and grandchild doings. Well, one summer day those boys got to thinking and they decided they wanted to do something nice for that grandmother that loved birds so much.

The problem those poor boys faced was they were crippled by being young and of little means to purchase something nice for Grandmother; that is to say, in an official capacity, those boys were flat-out broke. This was before the Labor Force had unionized and therefore any of the work they did was done *'in lieu of payment'*—that is lawyer-speak for saying those boys didn't make diddle-squat for their work.

Grandmother would probably really appreciate receiving a nice brooch with a bird picture in it or a sculpture of an eagle soaring above a desert plain. Both good ideas, but alas, with zero dollars funding those purchases, other ideas would need to be explored by those flat-out broke boys. Those boys thought about commissioning a painting, or a drawing of a bird, maybe that would suffice? However, their talents on the liberal arts front were about as deep as their pockets. The commissioning of the painting produced nothing more than images of yellow or blue globs of paint roosting in what appeared to be a very large fork...or maybe that was a tree? Regardless, it was a useless endeavor if ever there was one.

At long last, an enterprising idea was hit upon by Number 1, the boys' intellectual leader. Number 1 typically came up with the ideas and the rest of the boys followed, regardless of how good or bad his plans sounded. This current plan being formed from Number 1 would cost those boys zero dollars and would not require them the indignity of displaying their lack of talent in the field of arts and crafts. It was a plan everyone could get behind.

Grandmother liked birds, this point has been belabored enough by now, but Grandmother especially liked to hear birds sing. The one real big problem with birds is that they are a lazy species. Birds rise early in the morning, sing for a few hours, and then zip it. Those pretty singing birds call it a day quite early; they pack it in, as they say. "Hey bird, it's 10 in the morning, sing me that song you were singing at 6am?" Bird: "No can do man, it's way past quitting time. I work from 5:25 am to 7:59am, and not a minute over." This is how birds are, this is their line of thinking, which would also explain why they have yet to put together a functioning economy.

The typical bird day consists of singing for a few hours, gathering some sticks and straw to build a nest, eating a few worms, and then what? Nobody knows for sure what birds actually do for the remainder of the day; one could surmise there is a lot of sitting around done by the birds, pure laziness to be honest. The Bible calls this type of lazy behavior one of the seven deadly sins, denoted as "sloth". Those birds would be wise to start doing a little something lest they get on the wrong side of the big man upstairs.

This background information on bird society is vitally important to the idea that was rattling around in the brain of Number 1. Number 1 thought to himself, if we are these nice little boys we claim to be, then maybe...just maybe, we should make a recording of those beautiful birdsongs for our loving grandmother. This would show her how much we really care. And honestly, what says *'I love you'* more than a homemade production of the songs that birds sing? Nothing, that's what.

It was the boy's thinking that with this tape recording, Grandmother could press play on her audio-cassette player (which she did not own) and listen to those pretty little birds at any given time of the day. Think of the joy, think of the happiness. This idea had legs and merit, and most importantly, it came with a very attractive price tag: zero dollars.

The boys imagined that once the tape recording was made, whenever Grandmother and her sister Birdie got together, they could just sit and listen to that tape while playing pinochle, rummy, or whatever card game it is that old people always play. Those two bird lovers surely would be over the moon with happiness—you could almost say they would be as happy as a lark, which is a kind of bird.

Grandmother could even listen to that bird recording while she was decorating her Christmas tree with bird ornaments, maybe taking a break from decorating every once in a while to paint a picture of a bird. The idea of Grandmother decorating her Jesus tree with birds, painting birds on canvas, and listening to birdsongs all at once...this right here is the apex for a bird lover. This is the top of the heap as far as good ideas go, this is what they call in the business world *'bringing it all together'*. And so, those boys set out to make themselves a bird recording of actual real life birds so that Grandmother could *'bring it all together'*.

Being the sneaky boys they were, they wanted this to be a surprise for Grandmother. Therefore, they were to rely on themselves to get those lazy birds into the studio and make themselves a homemade recording. The studio in this case being the woods behind the lake house. Those birds in the forest behind the lake house sing like their little lives depend upon it, really belting out the tunes. The lake house is prime birdsong-recording real estate, if there ever was such a thing.

Eventually the opportunity arose. Grandmother was staying the weekend at the lake house, the recording would be made and distributed that very weekend. There was no time to delay. Those industrious little boys decided to set an alarm for 5am to catch those lazy, pretty singing birds. In case you have no idea on the subject matter, getting four little boys to set an alarm for themselves at 5am is no small potatoes. This task of alarm-setting at 5am essentially allows any one of those boys to be canonized by the Pope on account of this is an actual miracle recognized by the Holy Roman Catholic Church. Jesus Christ himself, at the moment those four boys all rose that morning at 5am, sat up in astonishment and said to himself, "Jesus Christ, well would you look at that, four little saints." This is paraphrased of course; Jesus would have actually said, "Me, well would you look at that, four little saints."

There those little boys were at 5am, quietly…stealthily…sneakingly sliding down the stairs of the lake house and into the chilly morning air of the outdoors. In the outdoors where all those pretty birds were singing their little brains out. The morning air was cold and those knobby knees were really put to work, shaking and such. The boys had not put too much thought into this idea as they still wore their pajamas; little more than shorts and t-shirts. The boys looked like a cluster of newborn foals, with those knobby knees and their shaking. Lots of shaking going on with those skin-and-bones boys on account of having zero percent body fat and just wearing shorts and t-shirts.

The boys crouched down for warmth, tape recorder at the ready. The birds were bringing their A-game that morning, really belting out some solid tunes, almost as if they knew they were going to be recorded. The eldest sibling, Number 1, the ringleader of this here production, prepared to give the signal to begin recording. Number 1 was always very official in manners such as this, a consummate professional. He directed his stagehands as though this were an actual studio recording. Number 1 count down, "and we're rolling in 5…4…3"…2…1….(the numbers 2 and 1 of course were silently counted on his hands, this was a professional production after all). The recording starts, and the archived transcript is as follows:

Bluejay#1: tweet-tweet-tweety-tweet

Cardinal: beep-tweet-tweet-beep
Bluejay#2: tweety-tweety-tweet-tweet
Bluejay#1: tweet-tweet-tweety-tweet
Crow: CAW CAW CAW CAW
Mourning Dove: who..who...who...I'm not an owl...who...who....please respect me for who I am..who..who
Bluejay#2: tweet-tweet
Crouched down boy with knobby knees: ffffffffffuuuuurrrrt...furtt..fuurrrrt
Other crouched down boys with knobby knees: (stifled giggling sounds...more stifled giggling)
END TRANSMISSION

The tape recording was stopped and the laughter exploded from those little boys with shaking knees. One of those little boys with shaking knees had let'er fly on the recording; passed gas, as they say if they are being polite on the subject. With all that crouching over and shaking of the knees, it was only a matter of time before one of those gassy bubbles found its way out of the intestinal maze, and one of those boys just could not hold it back. Recording or no recording, the gas was coming out of the maze.

Who was the perpetrator? Which boy had let'er fly? Nobody knows for sure, it simply doesn't matter. What does matter is that there was no going back after that. A second attempt was made to record those pretty singing birds, but what with all the giggling it was a pointless attempt; all that could be heard on the subsequent recording was giggling with birds in the background This was true for the third and fourth attempts as well.

Those gassy little boys with their shaking knobby

horse-knees had to go with the material they had. There is only so much time you can spend in the studio. It was the fart-interrupted bird recording or nothing, and so they went with it. The material they had was two minutes of real life birds tweeting and singing their little brains out followed by a five-second gas passing, followed by 30 seconds of giggling before Number 1 finally shut down the whole operation.

So that was that, those boys took that recording and presented it straight-faced to their adoring grandmother the very second she woke up that morning, curlers still firmly placed in her silver hair. The grandmother thought the gesture to be very sweet, intently listening to those singing birds...right up until the moment of the breaking of wind.

"Oh my," said Grandmother, and then the giggling returned that eventually turned into full-on fits of laughter. A very interesting way to start the day.

The recording those boys made had a very personal feel to it, a rawness that a recording from *National Geographic* could never capture in a million takes, and their grandmother loved every minute of it. Way better than any brooch with a bird picture in it, that's for sure.

BASKETBALL

Like most God-fearing Indiana families, the folks in that normal house liked basketball. To use the word 'liked' in that last sentence might be an understatement to say the least. A more correct sentence would be to say something along the lines of: those folks in the normal house worshipped at the altar of basketball. Jesus was a clear first when it came to worshipping, but basketball was nipping at old Jesus Christ's heels, a very close second in the order of worshipping. The boys with those knobby knees played basketball year round. Now this doesn't mean that the family suddenly gained wealth and built an indoor basketball court, lord no. Those boys played basketball outside year round, in the elements.

Those boys had adopted the mantra of the postman; that is to say, they delivered basketball greatness, come rain, sleet, hail, snow, or heat. It simply did not matter to those boys; -5 degrees was the same as 105 degrees. The only difference was the number of layers of clothing and how muddy those boys were going to get slopping around out there on the old hardwood—or concrete pad as it were. If there was light outside, the basketball games would be played, and sometimes those games were played even if there was no light. It was basketball, 24/7, 364; they usually took Christmas off out of respect for the big man's birthday.

The interesting thing about the family basketball court was that the out-of-bounds line underneath the basket was a drainage ditch. Not a large, industrial-sized drainage ditch, heavens no. This was a nice, modest-sized drainage ditch. The family didn't want to rub it into the neighbors' faces that they possessed a drainage ditch, therefore, the ditch was kept to a modest size; the family was very polite in that manner. They weren't drainage ditch-rich, but they were drainage ditch-well off, if there is such a thing.

The thing with the drainage ditch was, it almost always seemed to be full of water, or at least mud. The drainage ditch was very good at its single purpose on this here green earth: drain water. The drainage ditch posed a problem though. While it was good at being a drainage ditch, it was very bad at being an out-of-bounds line. If one of those boys with knobby knees happened to toss up an air ball, which they were known to do, that basketball that missed the rim, and the net, and the concrete pad? That basketball was coming down with a smack, right into the mud that the drainage ditch was storing.

Eventually those boys learned this lesson and when a shot looked as if it was going to fall short of hitting the rim, they would scatter. Instead of going for a rebound, they would scatter and scream their little heads off. This would play out like a scene from a war movie where the enemy had lobbed a grenade into a group of soldiers. If an air ball went up, you better hit the road. Duck for cover, lest you get splattered with mud, or gunk, or whatever else was lurking in the drainage ditch at the present moment. This also meant that the basketball was more often than not covered in water, or mud as it were.

All this cold basketballing, and water, and mud posed a very large problem to those boys, specifically in the months when basketball should not be played outside; like December and January. Those boys got cold, wet, numb hands. It shouldn't have to be told, but it's damn near impossible to hit a sweet floating jump shot when the hands you're using feel like two frozen ham hocks. Thinking about throwing a behind-the-back pass or trying a cross-over dribble move with those frozen hams for hands? Forget about it. Don't even try it.

Those cold hands killed the joy of backyard basketball. This turned backyard basketball into Bobby Knight basketball: crisp bounce passes, straight-up dribbling, and two-foot jump shots...no frills, no thrills. The late 1980s and early 1990s was the era of the UNLV Runnin' Rebels and the great Michael 'Air' Jordan—alley-oop slam dunks, fade-away jump shots, behind-the-back passes. Do you think those boys were interested in fundamentally sound, John Wooden-esk basketball? The short answer is 'no'. The long answer is 'hell no'.

The boys had tried playing basketball with their frozen ham-hock hands covered by mittens or ski gloves. However, the mittens and ski gloves only made the shooting and passing worse as they could no longer grip the ball. That basketball was flying everywhere, with the exception of the actual hoop where it was supposed to go. It was ridiculous— mittens and basketball? Come on, be for real. Just go inside and warm your pathetic little bones by the fire if you're going to try that again. Mittens and basketball go together like little boys and purple underwear with white seams, that is to say, they don't go together and should never be co-mingled. Lessons learned, move on.

And then those industrious little boys stumbled upon a discovery. A discovery aided and brought to you by a bronzed football star that played for the great city of Miami, Florida, located in the United States of America; where ironically, they don't know the first thing about playing basketball in the cold.

This bronzed football star was none other than the great Miami Dolphins football quarterback named Daniel Marino. In the late 1980s, Daniel Marino was lighting up the National Football League with his impressive footballing skills, which included passing the football for five hundred million yards.

But you see, Daniel Marino had a problem. While Mr. Marino played football in Miami, Florida, he was originally born and raised in Pittsburgh, and Pittsburgh has some cold winter months. Daniel wanted to keep those very valuable hands of his warm in the winter months when he was back there in Pennsylvania visiting family. Furthermore, Daniel wanted to look fashionable yet sleek while keeping those hands warm on his visits back home.

Enter the solution for Daniel Marino: Isotoner Gloves. Did Daniel Marino like Isotoner Gloves? Yes, yes he did. It seems Daniel had taken a very fond liking to Isotoner Gloves...so sleek, so comfortable, so warm, what's not to like really? "And what's that you say old Danny Marino, almost like not wearing gloves at all?" Isotoner Glove sales went through the damn roof (this may or may not be a factual statement). Isotoners here, Isotoners there, Isotoners everywhere. People could not get enough of the Isotoner Gloves...so sleek, so comfortable, so warm. Can you blame them? Honestly, can you blame them? You cannot, and should not blame them.

This gluttonous supply of Isotoner Gloves was beyond big news for those boys that loved to play basketball in the dead of winter. As luck would have it, the family had just been bequeathed a large supply of Isotoner Gloves. Hell, every family in the United States fell into a treasure trove of Isotoner Gloves in the late 1980s. It's almost as if the United States Government air-dropped fifty pairs of Isotoners to every family in the country, free of charge. Some families had closets dedicated to nothing but Isotoner Gloves (this is hearsay but most likely accurate given the previous statements regarding the gluttonous supply of the product).

How the family from that normal house actually fell into their Isotoner Glove fortune is not important, but to say the family was Isotoner-rich would be somewhat of an understatement. In case the point has not permeated into your brain yet, Isotoners are a very sleek, very comfortable, very warm glove—and the family from the normal house was swimming in them.

Initially, the folks in management were unaware that their beautiful, sleek, Daniel Marino-sponsored Isotoner Gloves were being borrowed and used for slopping around in a game of outdoor basketball in mid-December. It didn't take long though for the questions to begin bubbling to the top as the Isotoner Glove inventory soon became caked in dried mud. The boys who used those gloves to protect their hands during basketball, typically stashed the mud-caked Isotoner Gloves right back in the drawer from whence they came after the basketballing was done. No need to clean them as they would be using them again tomorrow for the same purpose However, after awhile, the dried mud was really lessening the sheen of the once-sleek Isotoner gloves. Those mud-caked Isotoners would be a major embarrassment if anyone from the outside world was to ever inquire about viewing the family's Isotoner collection.

The mother in charge of the Isotoner inventory would retort to those boys, "I wish you boys wouldn't use those nice Isotoner Gloves for slopping around in the mud." To this request, the boys merely shrugged. This was not a hill that management folks were willing to die, or even fight on, and those boys knew it. So those boys played basketball all winter long, in the cold, dark of December and the sleet of January. With those sleek, comfortable, warm Daniel Marino-sponsored Isotoner Gloves on those little hands, they could play basketball damn well whenever they pleased, and God bless Daniel Marino for that.

THE BUS

Those poor little darling boys with the knobby knees were forced to ride the big yellow school bus every morning and every afternoon to and fro to school. Can you imagine the indignity? Those boys also had to walk to the end of the road to catch the school bus, waiting outside in the cold, the rain, the heat. In this, they were again just like the postman, always delivering, regardless of the conditions forced upon them by the cruelty that is Mother Nature. Only in this instance, they were not delivering the mail, they were delivering their little butts to the cold vinyl seats of the big yellow school bus.

Those boys would stand there waiting for the bus, shivering in the pitch black of winter or sweating in the humidity of a sweltering Indiana summer morning. Sometimes those boys waited five minutes, sometimes they waited thirty minutes. The school bus was always a gamble, might be early, might be late, might not even show up. This was the deal when riding school buses; it's what you sign up for.

Those boys would wait with the neighbor kids, an odd lot if ever there was one. One of the neighbor children trudged to the bus stop every morning sporting a Kool-Aid mustache, usually of the cherry variety. "Hey buddy, I think you forgot to shave your mustache again this morning," one of those boys with knobby knees would say to Kool-Aid Mustache. There was never a response for this comment, just a head nod from Kool-Aid Mustache to acknowledge the fact that he had indeed forgotten to shave his cherry Kool-Aid mustache.

The other children at the bus stop were from a family with one million kids. Like the old nursery rhyme about an old lady that lived in a shoe (with so many kids she didn't know what to). These kids that lived in the shoe didn't even go to the same school that Kool-Aid Mustache and the boys with knobby knees went to, but our bus let 'em on anyways. This was a throwback to the hitchhiking era of the 1960s.

"Hey bus driver, we live in that big shoe over there and we saw you were taking these kids to the public school...we were wondering if maybe we could hitch a ride to the private school?" "Sure, get on in," the bus driver would say. "I'm headin' that way anyhow."

So there they were, this odd band of misfits, standing and waiting for that big old bus. The school bus would arrive and onto those cold vinyl seats those little skinny behinds would scoot. The boys with knobby knees were early in the bus route so picking their seat assignments was absolutely crucial, because the further the school bus went along the journey, the closer that big yellow bus got to school, the more suspect the characters getting onto the bus got. So it was imperative that those boys got good seats, lest they have to sit next to some unsavory characters.

The school bus was similar to coach seating in the big tan van—no rules, no regulation, no oversight. Come as you are and do as you please. The only difference between the big tan van and the school bus was the clientele. The folks in the back of the school bus were real life wild people. Wild people in every sense of the word. Their hair was wild, their clothes were wild, their speech was wild. Some of these wild kids were even from the trailer park. The trailer park! Did you just read that?! Yes you did! The. Trailer. Park. A park built for trailers. Can you imagine that? Being up close and personal with some real life kids from the trailer park, talk about a life-changing experience for those kids from the country.

Those kids from the trailer park that rode the big yellow bus had taken some upper-level English classes, it had seemed. How else could there be an explanation for their craftiness and advanced use of the English language? Those trailer park kids had surely had some advanced training on cussing, because they were very up-to-date on the latest vulgar terminology and readily shared it with all other passengers on the big yellow bus who were within earshot. The boys' uncle, he that was a cussing master and that appeared regularly on the cover of *Cussing Quarterly*, would've been right at home on that yellow school bus, he would've fit in just fine. Heck, that old cussing uncle might have even picked up a new phrase or two from those wild kids from the trailer park.

In elementary school, all four of those boys from the normal house served tours of duty with the same fellow that steered the driving wheel of the big yellow school bus. The first name of the man at the big wheel was 'Willy'; his last name was never disclosed, but a decent guess would be that it was 'the Bus Driver'.

When Willy the Bus Driver was a younger lad, he had decided that there were two things he wanted to do with his time here on this great planet. Those two things were raise hogs and drive school buses, in that order. So, Willy the Bus Driver ran a hog farm for his real profession and just picked these bratty kids up as a side-gig, you know, to help make ends meet.

Willy had a uniform that he wore daily. It consisted of a sweat-stained white V-neck t-shirt and blue-jean overalls. If the weather called for it, he wore a black and red flannel over his standard t-shirt and overalls uniform. This was every day. Every damn day he wore this outfit. Judging by the smell, it can be surmised that Willy the Bus Driver did not go to his closet in the morning to pick out a nicely pressed, clean, white V-neck t-shirt every morning. That is to say, Willy the Bus Driver did not have a closet full of this uniform, no, he had just the one he wore on his back, day in and day out.

This man that controlled the steering wheel of the big yellow bus weighed in around 300 pounds and always had gray stubble sprouting on his face. (It seems there's not enough time to shave when you're running a hog farm and driving the big yellow bus.) Willy's elevated weight was on account of eating most of the pork that was produced on his farm; Willy loved him some bacon, ham hock, pig feet, and most definitely some pork chops. Willy the Bus Driver would've been a rich man if he hadn't consumed half of the pork products being produced at his farm; he was literally eating into his profits. Willy's aroma consisted of a mix of sweat, bacon, hog shit, and cheap whiskey.

Now Willy, to be perfectly honest, did not give a shit about anything. His penchant for whiskey most likely attributed to his lack of shit-giving. In the morning Willy had one mission and one mission only: get the kids to school. In the afternoon, Willy had one mission and one mission only: get the kids home. Now, you might be thinking to yourself, hey author, I think you omitted a word from Willy's morning and afternoon mantras. Maybe you are thinking to yourself that the author left the word 'safely' off the mission statement of old Willy the Bus Driver. Perhaps the author meant to say, "Willy had one mission, his mission was 'to get the kids to school safely'." If you are thinking these thoughts, I would politely ask you to return to the section regarding Willy's lack of shit-giving. Rest assured, this was not an error of omission.

Again, to repeat and summarize, Willy's mantras were simple, 'get the kids to school', 'get the kids home'. Try and keep up with the story here.

Every once in a while, Willy would take some action to prove to all those students aboard the big yellow bus that he honestly did not give a shit. A little reminder to all those passengers about who was in charge—on the streets they call this sort of act '*keepin' it real*'. Well, Willy was about to keep it real.

It was always difficult to pinpoint what would set Willy off. Maybe he had heard one too many cuss words from the trailer park kids or maybe Mrs. Willy the Bus Driver only made six pieces of bacon for breakfast instead of his customary 10 pieces that morning. Whatever the trigger, it was imperative to not be on the receiving end of Willy's wrath.

When one of those kids from the trailer park got out of line or tripped Willy's trigger, that old hog farmer would stop the big yellow bus dead in its tracks. He'd stop the bus right in the middle of the street—Willy did not give a shit about blocking traffic. Willy's face, pounding red, would wrinkle and contort into an unimaginable ugliness...a frown a mile long would elongate his chubby face. Willy, covered in day-old whiskey sweat, would be snarling and drooling like Old Yeller (Old Yeller after he was sick with the crazy foaming-mouth disease).

He'd rise out of his big busdriver seat and storm down the bus aisle, like a trapped bull in the streets of Pamplona...only one way to go. Willy the bull would make his way to the offender and throw them into a different seat, or sometimes into a completely different section of the bus. Physically pick up those little butts and toss them into a different section of the bus. Can you imagine that? Can you even imagine it? Pray for your soul if you inadvertently had a leg, arm, or any other part of your body in the aisle as the bull bore down on the offending trailer park kid. Willy was a bull in every sense of the word. A hard-charging, flannel-wearing, whiskey- and bacon-smelling bull, and he was coming through, regardless of who, or what, was in his way.

Willy's lack of giving a shit was not confined to putting whoopings on little trailer park kids. Willy also did not care or give any credence to the laws of the road. Willy drove a big yellow bus that weighed five tons. Laws? Are you kidding me right now? Willy the Bus Driver and his big yellow school bus was the law.

Aside from stopping in the middle of the road for the sole reason of beating trailer park children, Willy committed other grave offences that would give traffic officers the shakes. Willy once committed a hit-and-run on some parked vehicles with a bus full of children. He scraped that big yellow bus right alongside a row of parked cars...like a bear scratching its back on some poor, unsuspecting tree. Do you think Willy cared? Do you think the word "oops" even crossed into Willy's brain? Those little passengers just sat there in stunned silence.

The law was on Willy's side on this accident, on account of Willy was the law. The mantra lived on, 'get the kids to school', 'get the kids home', at all costs. Willy was too tired from working on the hog farm to care about those cars he had sideswiped. Willy and his big yellow bus are the law, the parked cars were probably at fault in Willy's mind. Willy the Bus Driver needed to get home, he had a farm full of hungry hogs that needed fed, and lady cows with swollen teats that Willy's big sausage-like fingers needed to wrap around to ease that milk out. Willy did not have time for accidents. He's not going to stop for some two-bit car accident that wasn't his fault anyways. 'Get the kids to school.' This was Willy, this was the big yellow school bus.

All four of those boys served their tours of duty with Willy the Bus Driver admirably; they kept their mouths shut and their noses down and they made it out in one piece. They all lived to tell the horror stories, which cannot be said for some of those poor trailer park kids that were tossed along the way. Rest in peace, mouthy trailer park kids...rest in peace.

THE COLA WARS

We had neighbors back there in the normal house. Most folks have neighbors; it's one of the deals you sign on to when you participate in life on the big blue planet. Some neighbors are good, some neighbors are bad; all neighbors are weird in their own little ways. And your neighbors think your family is weird or quirky in your own little way. This is the deal, this is how it works. Everyone else is weird, but not you, you're normal...always have been, always will be.

Our neighbors in the normal house were very neighborly. They lived close to us and therefore qualified to be our neighbors, and we qualified to be theirs. This is the one and only qualification for being neighbors; you have to live by each other. Therefore, by default, we qualified.

The neighbors that were similar to the old lady that lived in a shoe had cranked out enough babies to put the Labor Force to shame; the exact number is unknown but is estimated to be roughly around one million babies, give or take a hundred thousand. The below chart lends credence to the sheer disparity of the neighbors kid population compared to that of the Labor Force.

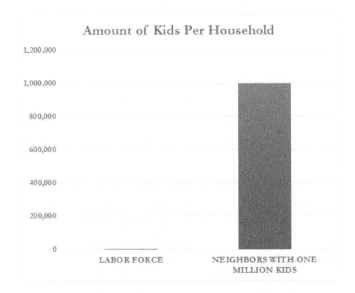

Amount of Kids Per Household

Now these neighbors had gotten out of the baby-making industry but they had saved the best baby for last. The last child in the lineage went by the name *Moo-Caca*. This obviously was not the formal name of the child—that would be ridiculous. People from the neighborhood gave their children good, Bible names, like Number 1 and Number 3. Moo-Caca's real name was Number 1,000,000; but he went by this ridiculous nickname because that's the only phrase that he uttered until he was roughly 15 years of age. A very strange child in this manner.

If you translate 'moo-caca' from 'baby speak' to English, it means chocolate milk. Apparently the boy's appetite for the substance was insatiable and could never be completely fulfilled. While initially 'moo-caca' meant chocolate milk, the older Moo-Caca grew, the phrase 'Moo-Caca' eventually became used to encompass anything and everything in that little boy's world.

"Hey little boy, what do you want to be when you grow up?" "Moo-Caca," came the reply. "Hey Moo-Caca, what's the surface of Jupiter composed of?" "Moo-Caca," he would say. This was the reply for any and every question, every opinion, every random thought that entered this child's mind. Moo-Caca this, Moo-Caca that, Moo-Caca everything, that's how it was, get it?

So Moo-Caca had one million siblings, one father, and one very tired mother. Moo-Caca's father worked for the soft drink company Coca Cola. This meant that everything in Moo-Caca's house was Coca Cola-themed; Coca Cola drinking glasses, Coca Cola Christmas ornaments, Coca Cola toilet bowl cleaners. Coca. Cola. Everything. The family even had a Coca Cola vending machine in their garage which dispensed free Coca Cola. This vending machine was never taken advantage of by the neighbor kids...except in that it was taken advantage of constantly. Free sodas for everyone, as long as you don't mind a little trespassing or breaking and entering.

The folks in the normal house thought their neighbors were weird on account of their one million inhabitants and their penchant for a Coca Cola-themed life. Moo-Caca and his family thought the folks in the normal house were weird on account of the mullet hairstyle the boys with knobby knees so proudly adorned. This was the mid-to-late 1980s so the mullet hairstyle was perfectly within the realm of normalcy in society, but Moo-Caca and his family seemed to take a strong disliking to the style.

Some of the boys from the normal house embraced the mullet hairstyle; some of the boys did not. Number 4 did more than embrace the style, he embodied it. Number 4 had a beautiful, flowing mullet with a spike on top. Numbers 1, 2, and 3 were envious, almost spiteful, of Number 4's beautiful mullet. Those other boys became so envious of Number 4's mullet that they eventually parted ways with their own mullets to spare the shame of having to stand next to the mullet master. Number 4's mullet was perfect in every manner. The wisps of his blondish-white mullet locks bouncing up and down as he ran. On sunny days, Number 4's mullet would reflect the sun rays just right and you could swear you were staring at redneck heaven...even if just for a split second. Number 4's mullet was so perfect, he would definitely be featured on the cover of *Mullet Monthly*, if any such publication were ever printed.

Moo-Caca's father, the weird one with a million babies, would taunt those boys regarding their flowing mullets and the beauty that radiated from their hair. The neighbor man would call those mullet-laden boys "cute little girls." His taunting was constant and very poignant. The neighbor man's taunting against the boys with knobby knees was most likely for three reasons and three reasons only. Reason one was because he was jealous of their beautiful hair, especially Number 4's; what balding middle-aged man wouldn't be? Reason two was because the boys looked like little girls, what with their skinny legs and flowing hair, and so the neighbor man was just *'calling it like he sees it'*, as the saying goes.

Reason three was because of the boys' role in the Cola Wars—the fallout from that cannot be understated.

Things were clicking right along there in the neighborhood for a good number of years. The folks in the normal house were being weird with their newfangled mullet hairdos, and the folks in the house with one million inhabitants were most certainly being weird, what with one million people living there. But one day, the wind in the neighborhood blew in a different direction. The wind blew differently and with that different wind, a new family arrived in the neighborhood. A new family from the city, city-slickers as it were. These city-slickers did things differently; they did things in a city-type manner, whatever in the world that means. One of the city-slicker children tried to use his rollerblade skates on our gravel street, and all the neighbors just stood and stared, dumbfounded by this city-slicker behavior.

The city family, like the family with one million inhabitants, also had a father that distributed beverages, one of those beverages being Pepsi Cola. The writing was on the wall; this was going to be a bit of a problem in the neighborhood. Apparently, the old neighborhood was not big enough for two soda distributors.

Initially things in the neighborhood were calm, but eventually word got out that there were two very clear sides forming: Coca Cola vs Pepsi. The Cola Wars began taking shape. Both sides slowly started sizing each other up; pushing, prodding, poking each other. Both sides explored how committed their adversary was to their cola cause. The two sides moved to shore up alliances within the neighborhood, and that's where the folks from that normal house come into the conversation.

The normal house with the four boys and their knobby knees represented a population boon to either side of the Cola Wars. But, which side of the Cola Wars did the normal house come down on? The simple answer is neither. The complicated answer is both. The normal house folks were technically on the side of Faygo, or RC Cola, or 'whatever is on sale' knock-off brand cola. Faygo? Can you believe that? RC Cola? What does that even mean? RC? I can tell you that RC most certainly does not stand for 'Really-good Cola'. These were the cheapest sodas ever created on this here green earth. So cheap the cardboard cases the soda came in would fall apart if you touched them wrong. The boys from the normal house were the de-facto Switzerland of the Cola Wars, never fully committing to or choosing a side.

The Switzerland of the Cola Wars had a dark side though. Those Switzerland boys would whore themselves out to either side of the Cola Wars that was willing to fill their little bellies full of free sugary soda. Back in those days, the normal house was on a fairly strict soda rationing program. You cannot expect folks in management to pony up big bucks just so those little boys can drink all the soda they want, this was most definitely not an option. Those boys from the normal house had to get their soda fixes elsewhere, on the black market. And due to the escalating tensions of the Cola Wars, the black market was awash in cola-flavored soda. Therefore, when the neighbor kids involved in the Cola Wars would offer soda for loyalty, those boys from the normal house would jump right in.

"Hey old buddy, old pal, what's say you crack open that big old bottle of Pepsi Cola and let's get this party going!" the boys from Switzerland would say. The neighbor kids gladly obliged; their households were under no such rationing and they were eager to get folks on their side...the right side of the Cola Wars. When you are fighting a war, you cannot afford to be stingy with the one thing most near and dear to the war efforts, which was cola-flavored soda.

The Cola Wars finally came to a head when the Pepsi Cola folks lured Moo-Caca and his older brother, Number 985,592, into their headquarters under the guise of friendship. To the uncommitted Switzerland boys, it appeared the Cola Wars tensions were possibly easing. Relationships were being mended between the old adversaries, soon we would all celebrate and embrace our differences and agree to live peacefully with one another. It was a utopian dream coming true...or so the boys from the normal house thought.

In reality, the Pepsi Cola kids had not invited Moo-Caca and his brother over for fun, it was all a ruse; which is to say it was a cunning lie. Once all those kids began playing and having fun, one of those Pepsi Cola kids innocently enough said that he was thirsty, a bit parched, if you will.

"Hey Moo-Caca," one of the Pepsi kids called out, "can you reach into our fridge there and grab me a cold soda?"

Moo-Caca naively made his way to the refrigerator and upon opening it, he froze dead in his tracks. What Moo-Caca saw was more Pepsi Cola than he knew even existed. Cases and cases of Pepsi Cola cans...the forbidden juice. "Mooooooooo-Caca," he whispered quietly to himself, which translates in English to "hoooooooly shit." Moo-Caca begrudgingly handed out some sodas and before long those boys from Switzerland and the Pepsi kids were slugging down soda like there was no tomorrow. Belly-aches be damned.

Finally, a Pepsi kid turned to Moo-Caca. "Hey Moo-Caca, why don't you have a sip?" Moo-Caca's older brother cried out in protest, "Don't do it Moo-Caca, that's Satan's juice!" The Pepsi kids and the Switzerland boys goading Moo-Caca on. Daring him to put that can to his lips and drink. And did Moo-Caca try that Pepsi Cola? Did Satan's juice touch his innocent little lips? Oh yes. Yes it did. Moo-Caca had tasted the forbidden juice, and Moo-Caca had liked it. He liked it way better than chocolate milk in fact.

The playdate was quickly halted on account of Moo-Caca's older brother and the fear that was welling up inside of him. Moo-Caca was not old enough to understand the ramifications of his little sip of Pepsi Cola, but his older brother fully understood. He understood they were in deep, deep shit. The pair fled back to their home, the home with one million inhabitants. They fled back to the protection of Coca Cola.

Upon entering their home, their father picked up on their scent, he smelled something funny in the air. After years of smelling nothing but the scent of Coca Cola, the father had developed a keen sense of smell for any non-Coca Cola soda. Immediately the father smelled the slight difference in fructose corn syrup ratios between his beloved Coca Cola and the much maligned Pepsi Cola. This was not a cola scent the father recognized, and that was bad. How bad it was is anyone's guess. What is known is that Moo-Caca and his older brother would not be seen for weeks following the incident. Perhaps they were sent to a Coca Cola bottling plant to spend some time on the production line to atone for their sins; this is merely speculation but certainly within the realm of possibility.

This event was the one and only shot fired in the Cola Wars. A single shot that signaled the beginning of the Cola Cold War. The two families remained at odds for years, neither allowed to enter the other's residence. Ronald Reagan and Mikhail Gorbachev's cold war couldn't hold a candle to the Cola Cold War. There was a no-cola zone established between the properties that neither family could enter while holding a cola-flavored soda. This zone helped maintain the peace in the neighborhood. The true Cola Cold War had begun and tensions would remain heightened for years.

This development of course was to the delight of the boys with knobby knees from the normal house. Those Switzerland boys had it even better during the Cola Cold War. Both sides made sure those little Swiss bellies stayed full of free soda. The Switzerland boys whoring themselves out to whoever was in a giving mood. Yes sir, those were good times, all the soda you can drink for a few seconds of loyalty. Mooooo-caca!

THE NORMAL HOUSE

The normal house was a good house, but as the old saying goes, all good things must come to an end. Eventually the normal house was sold by the family; however, the memories of the Labor Force, Cussing Game, and Cola Wars remain. The house was sold to some other folks that were probably weird and looking for some neighbors to be weird with.

The feature that finally sold the prospective buyers was the bathroom that was situated right next to the kitchen table. This bathroom allowed for the folks that were eating their breakfast, lunch, or dinner, to hear and smell everything that was occurring behind that thin bathroom door. No secrets going down in there, very similar to the pissing pot at the lake house. Nothing completes breakfast like hearing and smelling someone else's number two...nothing. This feature of the normal house sold those prospective buyers because it displayed to their soon-to-be visitors how well off they were. Those prospective buyers wanted all visitors to know that they were toilet-rich, just like we used to be.

ABOUT THE AUTHOR

As seen in the above picture, the author is a consummate professional, always has been, always will be. Born Matthew William Kent in Fort Wayne, Indiana, he was renamed 'Number 2' at an early age. He approaches his writing as he does everything in life, with a striped tie, extremely large pointed collars, and an overwhelming sense of professionalism. Growing Up Kent is the author's first foray into writing, depending upon how badly it flounders, there will be additional writings, or burning of manuscripts, depending upon the level of failing of this book.

ON THE COVER

The family poses for a quick picture prior to their weekly Sunday visit to the big man's house. The mother smiles as she looks towards the camera, completely oblivious to the fact that the father, who stands next to her with his 'shit-eating' grin, has put her little darling boys up to several pranks. The child to the far right has hiked his pants up as high as they possibly could go, his hand slid into his pocket to keep them at the optimum height for the picture. The child directly in front of mother has turned his pockets out, to signify that he is dead-broke. The youngest child, the one with the bow-tie is as lost as the mother, so he laughs, mostly because everyone else is. The child dressed in the flannel, business-casual shirt can no longer hold it together and begins laughing as the photo is taken. Three weeks later, when the mother takes the film to the local Keltsch Drug Store to get the film developed, she discovers her entire family has sold her out for a cheap laugh, such is life in the Kent household.

Made in the USA
Monee, IL
22 July 2021

74102740R00080